SOUTHWEST COMFORT FOOD

SOUTHWEST

Comfort FOOD

Slow and Savory

Marilyn Noble

RIO NUEVO
PUBLISHERS

Rio Nuevo Publishers®
P.O. Box 5250
Tucson, AZ 85703-0250
(520) 623-9558, www.rionuevo.com

We would like to thank Dusty and Bob Hudson for their gracious permission to photograph
this book at their home in the San Rafael Valley of Arizona.

Book design: Karen Schober Book Design, Seattle, Washington.
Printed in China.

10 9 8 7 6 5 4 3 2 1

Library of Congress Cataloging-in-Publication Data

Noble, Marilyn.
  Southwest comfort food : slow and savory / Marilyn Noble.
     p. cm.
  Includes bibliographical references and index.
  ISBN-13: 978-1-933855-32-5 (alk. paper)
  ISBN-10: 1-933855-32-0 (alk. paper)
1. Cooking, American--Southwestern style. 2. Cookbooks. I. Title.
  TX715.2.S69N63 2011
  641.5979--dc23
                    2011019293

Contents

Introduction

WHEN THE WORLD SEEMS TO BE SPINNING OUT OF CONTROL, what's the one thing to which people turn for solace? Food . . . comfort food, to be precise. Whether it's a steaming bowl of tomato soup or a big gooey plate of mac and cheese, comfort food connects us to a time when life was simpler and the problems of the world didn't seem so overwhelming and scary. It reminds us that no matter what, life's simple pleasures can be the most important.

Growing up in the southwestern U.S., I developed an appreciation for a hot flour tortilla wrapped around a mound of *refritos,* a spicy bowl of chili enjoyed while watching football with my dad and Uncle Bobby, and the wild game that my grandmother cooked after my grandfather's successful day of hunting. As I got older and began to travel and develop a more refined and adventurous palate, my sense of comfort food grew too. Cioppino reminds me of fun times in San Francisco, salmon baked on a cedar plank brings me back to beach cookouts in the Pacific Northwest, and then there's *gallo pinto,* the ubiquitous dish of Costa Rica that conjures up the many happy hours spent with my Tico friends in the jungle. So while many of the recipes in this book have their origins in the food traditions of the Southwest, some are just dishes that I love, that remind me that the phrase "comfort food" is as much about the pleasures of the table as it is about memories.

Many of the recipes in this book require some method of slow cooking, but that's one of the other key components of comfort food—it should be a complete sensory experience, and that includes the preparation.

In these days of multitasking, instant gratification, and microwaves, you might wonder why slow cooking would appeal to anyone. Who wants to plan dinner hours or even days in advance when you can make a quick stop at the store on the way home, buy something ready-made, and heat it up in the microwave as soon as you walk in the door? It's quick, it's easy, sometimes moderately tasty, and lets you get on to the next task at hand.

The fact is that slow cooking is about the art of preparing food. It requires advance planning, but the payoff is a sensory overload of enjoyment. Nothing is better on a cold winter day than the heady smell of a hearty stew simmering all afternoon on the stove or a succulent piece of beef braising in a bath of red wine, onions, and garlic. Slow cooking brings complexity to the flavor and texture of food and allows us to reconnect with its loving preparation. Slow cooking brings us back to a time when eating was more than just another task to check off the daily to-do list. It reminds us of family dinners, celebrations, and enjoying a hearty meal with loved ones. It brings us comfort.

THE AMERICAN SOUTHWEST IS BLESSED with an abundance of food-producing regions, from the cattle-grazing land in Texas to the agricultural breadbaskets of California, Arizona, New Mexico, and Colorado. In the Southwest, it's easy to find fresh, locally produced food almost everywhere. And then there's the natural bounty of nature. Hunting is a way of life in the Southwest, and many traditional game recipes have been handed down from the days of the early explorers and settlers.

Southwestern cuisine is a mélange of influences. From the original inhabitants, we get a plethora of dishes containing corn, beans, and squash. As newcomers settled, they brought their own cooking traditions, a trend that continues today as people migrate from other parts of the U.S. and from other countries. When the first Europeans came west, slow cooking wasn't a luxury; it was a way of life. Game meats were more palatable stewed over a slow fire, and for people who spent most of their waking hours working the land, either as farmers, ranchers, or miners, it was easier to put something in the pot at the beginning of the day and come in to a waiting hot meal at sunset.

Slow cooking is not only a celebration of the abundance that surrounds us; it connects us to our history and our culture. Today, even though we enjoy modern conveniences that speed up the task of preparing food, it's still nice to come home at the end of the day to a waiting hot meal.

Cooking Methods

BRAISING • A throwback to the days when our ancestors threw a piece of meat into a heavy pot with some vegetables and liquids, then buried it in hot coals to simmer away, modern braising is an easy, non-labor-intensive way to prepare a dish. All it takes is a heavy pot with a tight-fitting lid, a cut of meat or fish, some aromatic herbs and vegetables, some liquid such as wine or broth, and a slow temperature in the oven or on the stovetop. Braising tenderizes tougher, inexpensive cuts of meat and creates a complex blending of flavors.

The pot is the key to successful braising. It should be heavy to conduct heat evenly and slowly, and the top must fit tightly so the steam condenses and drips down over the meat, as opposed to escaping. The food should fit into the pot without a lot of excess room so more of the meat stays in contact with the braising liquid. My favorite braising pot is a Dutch oven made of enamel-covered cast iron.

The second key to good braising is the temperature. While some dishes lend themselves to stovetop braising, the best results for long, slow braising come from an oven heated to no more than 300 degrees F. The even heat surrounds the pot and allows the cook to leave the dish unattended for long periods. The liquid should simmer gently and not boil, which dries out and toughens the meat.

Braising involves three main steps. The first is browning the meat to add depth of flavor and color to the finished dish. If you're cooking small pieces, make sure you don't crowd them in the pan. If the pieces are too close together, the moisture gets trapped and they steam rather than brown. Also, the surface of the meat should be dry before you add it to the hot oil.

When the meat is browned, it's time to deglaze the pan. Add the braising liquid to the pan and bring it to a boil, scraping up the browned bits from the bottom. This adds layers of flavor to the finished dish.

After the dish has finished cooking, the sauce may need to be reduced. Remove the meat and/or vegetables and place the pan over medium heat to simmer the braising liquid until the volume is reduced and the flavors are concentrated. Pour the sauce back over the dish to serve.

BARBECUING ● This is not the same as grilling, the quick cooking of food over a hot open fire. Barbecuing requires a low fire and a long exposure to indirect heat. The art of barbecue is a much-debated and contested way of life for many people, but it doesn't have to be complicated. All it takes is a grill and lots of propane or charcoal.

If you use a gas grill, this generally means lighting one side of the burners and placing the meat over the other side with a foil drip pan beneath. If you use a charcoal grill, which I find preferable, use a charcoal chimney to light the coals. Pour them into the grill and arrange them in a circle around the edges. Place a foil drip pan in the center. Keep a coal or two in the chimney and fill it up again to keep plenty of coals ready to replenish the fire. Use a chimney as opposed to lighter fluid, which gives the food a chemical taste. I also like to use lump charcoal made from natural wood as opposed to briquettes that have added chemical binders in them.

The temperature should be low, between 250 and 275 degrees F, and it's important to not open the grill any more than you must while the meat is cooking. Each time you lift the lid, heat escapes and slows down the cooking time.

Exceptional barbecue requires four different components to keep the meat moist and add flavor:

The *slather* is a pasty marinade usually made with sugar, mustard, hot sauce, and other flavorings. Rub it into the meat and let it sit while the grill heats.

The *rub* is a dry seasoning sprinkled over the meat right before cooking.

The *mop* is liquid applied during cooking to tenderize the meat and keep it moist. Mops can consist of fruit juice or wine and be applied with a spray bottle or brush.

The *sauce* is the finishing touch and should be added after the cooking is complete. Because most barbecue sauces have a sugar base, applying them to the meat while it's still on the grill can cause the surface to burn. Apply the sauce after the meat comes off the grill, and then pass the extra for guests to add at their discretion.

SMOKING ● The difference between smoking and barbecuing is subtle, but when you smoke meat, you use wet wood chips to add flavor to the meat as it cooks. Smoking requires a lower temperature (200–225 degrees F) and a longer time, as much as 45 minutes to one hour per pound for roasts. You can smoke food on your grill, following the manufacturer's directions, or you can invest in a smoker. A smoker is handy if you want to do larger quantities of food such as fish or sausage.

ROASTING ● Roasting is done uncovered in the oven with dry heat and is good for many cuts of meat and vegetables. The oven temperature should never exceed 325 degrees F to give a brown exterior and a moist interior.

A few words about slow cookers

Also known as Crock Pots, slow cookers came into common use in the 1970s. The originals had two temperatures, low and high, and the crock and the heating element were one unit, making them a challenge to clean. Many of the recipes available then involved tough and inexpensive cuts of meat covered by canned soups or vegetables and cooked for hours. It was a convenient way to fix dinner, but with the emphasis on processed foods, not always healthy or tasty.

Today, slow cookers come with detachable ceramic crocks and adjustable timers and temperature controls. While you can still cook the old recipes if that's what satisfies your taste buds, it's easy to adapt other recipes for use in a slow cooker. Many braising recipes and most of those for soups and stews can be varied for Crock Pot cooking. While a slow braise in an oven will almost always give a superior result, if you want the convenience of putting a meal on to cook before you leave the house in the morning, you can easily do so with a modern slow cooker. Recipes in this book that adapt well to that kind of cooking will always offer a slow-cooker variation.

Ingredients

STOCK • The basic building block for many slow-cooked recipes is a meat or vegetable stock. You can buy canned stock, but you can almost as easily make your own and control the ingredients and resulting flavors. I usually plan a stock-making weekend several times a year. One day I make chicken and/or vegetable and the next I make beef. As I cook vegetables, I save parts that would otherwise go to waste, like asparagus and broccoli stems, stick them in a plastic bag in the freezer, and use them later to make vegetable stock. If you roast a turkey or chicken, the carcass makes a rich stock. One note: I don't recommend salting the stock when you make it because it becomes more difficult to control the flavor of the finished dish. Once you get in the habit of making it yourself, you'll never buy the canned product again.

MEATS • Beef, pork, poultry, lamb, game, and even buffalo are appropriate for slow cooking. The method you use depends somewhat on the cut of the meat. Tender, moist meats such as prime rib roasts and pork loins are generally conducive to roasting while less tender, less expensive cuts such as chuck roasts lend themselves to long, slow braising. Wild game, such as venison or pheasant, because it can be tough and strongly flavored, will almost always benefit from a long marinade and slow, moist cooking.

Buffalo or bison is becoming an increasingly popular red meat, largely because it has less fat and fewer calories than beef. Bison in the United States is always raised without antibiotics or hormones, and much of it is grassfed, which gives it a more natural flavor than feed-lot beef. In fact, for the highest quality meats, always look for the logo of the American Grassfed Association. According to AGA, products from grassfed animals include beef, bison, lamb, pork, poultry, eggs, and dairy products. A variety of research shows that meat, dairy products, poultry, and eggs from animals fed grass diets, rather than grain-based diets, are higher in beta carotene (Vitamin A), conjugated linoleic acid (CLA), and Omega-3 fatty acids. Initial research has shown all of these elements to be crucial in reducing cholesterol, diabetes, cancer, high blood pressure, and other life-threatening diseases. Research also shows grassfed products to be lower in fat and cholesterol and less likely to contain harmful *E. coli* bacteria.

VEGETABLES ● The best vegetables are those you either grow yourself or buy on Saturday morning at your local farmers market. They're usually fresh, sometimes organic, and grown within a few hours' drive of where you buy them. It's also fun to get to know your local food producers.

When produce is in season, make it a practice to buy extra to freeze for use later. If you don't have a big enough freezer, you can still buy frozen, out-of-season fruits and vegetables at your local grocery. They're much preferable to buying the canned, overly processed, and salted variety. The only exception is tomatoes—sometimes canned tomatoes are best for slow-cooked dishes.

Corn. Many dishes in this book call for corn in various forms. If a recipe calls for fresh corn, scrape it off the cob using a sharp knife. You may substitute frozen corn for fresh. Avoid canned corn, unless the recipe specifies it. Hominy, *nixtamal*, and posole all refer to dried corn kernels that have been soaked in an alkali water to remove the hulls. You can find them dried, frozen, or canned. The canned is the least desirable. See Sources on page 142 to locate the dried version.

Green Chiles. Many of the recipes in this book require roasted, peeled, and seeded green chiles. There are dozens of different varieties, with Anaheims being the mildest and most common. New Mexico chiles range from mild to very hot, and which you use depends on your own heat tolerance. Everywhere you travel in New Mexico in late summer and early fall you'll encounter the pungent scent of roasting chiles. At street-corner stands and in farmers markets, you'll hear the roar of the propane and the crackle of the skins as they spin in the roasters. Buy them in bulk and freeze them for use all winter.

To roast your own chiles, place them on a hot grill or under the broiler and turn frequently until the skin is blackened and blistered. Cover the roasted chiles with a damp towel for about 15 minutes to allow them to steam. Remove the peels, stems, and seeds and they're ready to use. If you want to save some for later, freeze with the peels on and remove them right before use. Avoid canned chiles unless you have no other options.

Red Chiles. New Mexico green chiles that are allowed to ripen on the vine turn bright red and become even hotter. They're usually dried; if you drive through Hatch, New Mexico, in the fall you'll see roofs full of red chiles drying in the sun. They're also tied into *ristras* or ground into chile powder.

Jalapeños. Usually green, but sometimes red, jalapeños are small, meaty peppers with varying degrees of heat, but usually on the hot side. They can be used fresh without peeling, but they need to have the seeds and white inner membranes removed by hand. Use disposable plastic gloves and take care not to scratch your nose or eyes.

Chipotles. Smoked and dried jalapeños, chipotles can be found in most grocery stores canned in *adobo* sauce. You can also find the dried version at some Mexican groceries or farmers markets. If you're ambitious, you can smoke and dry your own (page 87).

SEASONINGS ● A good rule of thumb for converting fresh herbs into dried is to use one teaspoon of dried for every tablespoon of fresh called for in the recipe. In many slow-cooking recipes, the two are interchangeable; however, if the herb is used to finish a dish, fresh is better and substituting the dried version will give you an inferior result.

Store your dried herbs and spices in airtight glass containers and don't keep them for more than a year. They lose their potency, which will affect the flavor of the dish. If you pinch a bit between your fingers and you don't get any aroma, it's time to buy a new bottle.

Chile Powders. Always use pure chile powder. Be careful when you buy it at the grocery store—some common brands have added salt, cumin, garlic powder or other additives that will affect the end result of your dish. Chile powder comes in different heats, so choose the one that appeals to you. Some recipes, such as that for *mole*, require several different kinds of powder from different chile varieties. If a recipe doesn't specify, just use your favorite. I like those from Hatch and Chimayo, New Mexico, the best.

Store the fresh powder in a dark cupboard in an airtight container. Replace it if you notice the color changing or when the aroma fades. It's not dangerous—it just won't give you any flavor.

Oils. Always use extra-virgin olive oil. Anything that's labeled just "olive oil" probably contains chemically refined oil and may have impurities. Because olive oil has a strong flavor and a low smoke point, it's not always the first choice for every recipe. Organic, expeller-pressed canola oil and grapeseed oil are both good options for frying, or whenever you need a light oil with an unobtrusive flavor.

The most important ingredient for comfort food cooking, or any cooking for that matter, is one you won't find listed in any recipe. That's love, and it's why Grandma's Sunday pot roast or Mom's special chili evoke such warm memories. Most of us grew up in homes where the cooks were not *Cordon Bleu* chefs, but we still look back on those dinners with a touch of nostalgia and longing for the old days. I hope you'll use this book as a way to create and celebrate your own traditions, keep those old memories alive, and build new ones for your family and friends.

Basics

| *Beef Stock*

1 ½ pounds lean stew beef

4 quarts water

1 large yellow onion, chopped

2 carrots, chopped

1 leek, white and light green portions, chopped

2 celery ribs, including tops, chopped

10 black peppercorns

1 bay leaf

Always keep beef broth on hand in the freezer to flavor gravies, soups, and stews. Freeze it in an ice-cube tray and then place the cubes in a plastic freezer bag for easy use in gravies, or freeze in one-quart bags to use in soups and stews.

Place the stew meat in a large stockpot and add water. Bring to a boil over high heat, skimming the foam from the surface. Reduce heat to low. Add the onion, carrots, leek, celery, peppercorns, and bay leaf. Simmer uncovered over low heat for 4 hours. Remove from heat and allow to cool for 30 minutes. Strain into a bowl, discarding the solids, and then cover and refrigerate. When the fat has solidified on the surface, skim it off and discard. Keep refrigerated for use within 1 week, or freeze and use within 3 months.

| *Vegetable Stock*

2 russet potatoes, cut into 1-inch cubes

2 large yellow onions, coarsely chopped

2 carrots, chopped

2 turnips, chopped

2 celery ribs, tops included, chopped

1 small head cabbage, chopped

4 quarts water

8 black peppercorns

1 bay leaf

Another freezer essential, you can use any combination of vegetables you have on hand, but unless you're making a specific soup, avoid strongly flavored vegetables such as broccoli, cauliflower, and asparagus.

Add vegetables to a large stockpot and cover with water. Bring to a boil over high heat. Add peppercorns and bay leaf, then reduce heat to low, cover, and simmer for 1 hour. Remove from heat and allow to cool for about 30 minutes. Strain into a bowl and refrigerate for use within 1 week, or freeze for use within 3 months.

| MAKES 2 QUARTS | Brown Veal Stock |

Oil

10 pounds veal bones

8 quarts water

2 medium-size onions

6 medium-size carrots

6 celery ribs

4 leeks

1 teaspoon black peppercorns

2 bay leaves

2 sprigs fresh thyme

8 garlic cloves, pressed

½ cup tomato paste

This takes several hours but is well worth it when you need to make a rich demi-glace or even braise vegetables. Ask for veal bones at your local meat market or at a high-end grocery store with a gourmet meat department.

Preheat the oven to 450 degrees F. Oil (canola preferred) a roasting pan big enough to hold the bones in a single layer, or use two pans if necessary.

Remove the meat from the bones and arrange the meat and bones in a single layer in the prepared roasting pans. Roast in the oven until dark brown, about 1–1 ½ hours, turning to brown all sides and avoid burning.

Transfer the bones and meat to a large stockpot or kettle, 12- to 14-quart. Siphon the fat from the roasting pan(s) and discard. Deglaze the roasting pan(s) with 1 cup water, scraping up the browned bits, and then add to the kettle. Cover the bones and meat with 8 quarts of water or enough to cover by 3 inches. Bring to a boil and then reduce heat to very low so that the water barely simmers. Cook uncovered for 10 hours, skimming the foam and adding more water as necessary to keep the bones covered.

Meanwhile, cut the onions into quarters and the carrots and celery into 1-inch chunks. Trim the leeks and wash well. Oil a large roasting pan and arrange the vegetables in a single layer. Place in the oven and roast for 30 minutes or until browned. Remove from the oven, cool, and then cover and chill.

After the bones have simmered for 10 hours, add the roasted vegetables to the stock along with the peppercorns, bay leaves, thyme, garlic, and tomato paste. Return to a simmer and cook for another 2 hours. Remove from heat and cool about 1 hour.

Strain the stock in batches through a metal sieve, pressing the solids to extract all of the liquid. Discard the solids. Chill for several hours uncovered. Remove and discard the layer of fat.

Bring the stock to a boil over high heat, then lower heat and allow to simmer gently for about 1 hour until reduced to 2 quarts. Remove from heat and allow to cool, then cover and chill. Keeps up to 1 week refrigerated or 3 months frozen.

MAKES 3 QUARTS | *Chicken Stock*

1 stewing chicken, whole or cut up

4 quarts water

1 large yellow onion, chopped

2 carrots, chopped

2 celery ribs, tops included, chopped

8 black peppercorns

1 bay leaf

Chicken stock is a basic to always keep in the freezer. Shred the meat from the chicken and freeze it for use in soups, salads, or enchiladas.

Remove the skin and fat and rinse the chicken. Place in a large stockpot and cover with water. Add the vegetables. Bring to a boil over high heat. Skim the foam from the surface and reduce heat to low. Add peppercorns and bay leaf and simmer uncovered over low heat for 3 hours. Remove from heat and allow to cool for about 30 minutes. Remove the chicken parts, then strain the stock into a bowl. Cover and refrigerate. When fat has solidified on the surface, skim it off and discard. Keep refrigerated for use within 1 week, or freeze and use within 3 months.

Smoked-chicken Stock

MAKES 1 ½ QUARTS

1 smoked-chicken carcass
1 large onion, chopped
2 ribs celery
8 cups water
10 peppercorns

After you've barbecued a chicken, save the meaty bones for this stock that adds a slightly smoky flavor to soups and stews.

Place chicken bones, onion, and celery in a large stockpot. Add water and bring to a boil over high heat. Skim the foam from the surface and add pepper. Reduce heat to low and simmer uncovered for 3 hours. Remove from heat and cool at room temperature for 30 minutes. Remove chicken bones and strain the stock into a bowl. Refrigerate for use within 3 days or freeze for use within 3 months.

Seafood Stock

Shell from 1 lobster tail

Shells from 1 pound of shrimp

4 quarts water

½ pound white fish, such
as halibut

1 medium yellow
onion, chopped

2 celery ribs, including
tops, chopped

¼ cup Italian
parsley, chopped

½ cup dry white wine

1 teaspoon black peppercorns

*A flavorful addition to risottos, stews, or any other dish that requires
a delicate seafood essence.*

Place lobster and shrimp shells in a large stockpot, then cover with water.
Bring to a boil over high heat. Skim foam from surface, then reduce heat to
low. Add fish, onion, celery, parsley, wine, and pepper. Cover and simmer
gently over low heat for 45 minutes. Remove from heat and allow to cool at
room temperature for 30 minutes. For a more pronounced fish flavor,
leave the shells and fish in the cooling broth. For a lighter flavor, remove
before cooling. Strain the broth into a bowl and refrigerate. Use within 3
days or freeze for up to 3 months.

Simmer

SERVES 8 | *Vegetable Barley Soup*

¾ cup pearl barley

12 cups vegetable stock or water

2 tablespoons extra-virgin
olive oil

I large onion, chopped

4 carrots, chopped

2 celery ribs, chopped

I cup thinly sliced mushrooms

I large zucchini, diced

I can (14 ½ ounces each)
chopped tomatoes with juice

2 bay leaves

Salt and pepper

A satisfying vegetarian soup for an early fall dinner. Serve with warm French bread.

In a large saucepan, combine the barley with 3 cups of vegetable stock or water. Bring to a boil over medium heat, cover, reduce heat to low and simmer for I hour or until the liquid is absorbed.

Meanwhile, heat the olive oil in a large Dutch oven or stockpot and add the onion, carrots, and celery. Cover and cook the vegetables for about 5 minutes or until soft. Add the mushrooms and zucchini and stir until soft, another 2 minutes or so. Add the tomatoes, bay leaves, and remaining vegetable stock and simmer 30 minutes, covered. Add the barley and simmer 5 minutes more. Add salt and pepper to taste and ladle into bowls.

SERVES 6

Black Bean Soup

1 pound dry black beans

Water to cover

1 bay leaf

1 large onion, minced

3 cloves garlic, chopped

2 jalapeños, seeded and chopped

1 teaspoon salt

½ teaspoon black pepper

1 cup chicken or vegetable stock

Sour cream, for garnish

Cilantro, chopped, for garnish

Soaking the beans overnight softens them and eliminates the gas, but if you're in a hurry, cover with water, bring them to a boil, then remove from heat, cover, and allow to soak for an hour.

Rinse the beans and sort to remove any dirt or small rocks. Rinse again in cold running water. Place the beans in a large bowl and cover with cold water. Allow to soak 8 hours.

Drain and rinse the beans again and place in a stockpot. Cover with fresh water and bring to a boil. Add bay leaf, onion, garlic, and jalapeños. Cover, reduce heat, and cook until tender, approximately 1 ½ hours.

When the beans are tender, remove from heat and stir in salt, pepper, and chicken or vegetable stock. Use an immersion blender to puree the mixture, or add in batches to a food processor or blender. If the soup is too thick, add more stock to thin. Reheat to serving temperature. Ladle into bowls and garnish with a dollop of sour cream and a sprinkle of cilantro.

Slow Cooker Variation: Place the soaked beans in the slow cooker with enough water to cover. Add the bay leaf, onion, garlic, and jalapenos. Cook on high for 4 hours, or on low for 6 hours. Add the salt, pepper, and stock and cook for another 30 minutes on high. Puree and serve, adding more stock to thin, if necessary. Garnish with sour cream and cilantro.

SERVES 6 | ## Sopa de Frijoles

I pound dried kidney beans

Water to cover

8 cups vegetable stock

I large onion, minced

2 cloves garlic, minced

I teaspoon dried
Mexican oregano

2 teaspoons salt

3 tablespoons extra-virgin
olive oil

½ cup tomato sauce

2 tablespoons red wine vinegar

6 mint leaves, finely chopped

Croutons, for garnish

Always allow the beans to cook for a while before adding salt. Adding the salt too soon makes the beans tough.

Wash and sort the beans well. Soak overnight in cold water. Drain and add to a large stockpot. Cover with the vegetable stock and add the onion, garlic, and oregano. Bring to a boil over high heat, then reduce heat to low, cover, and simmer for I to I ½ hours or until beans are soft. Add the salt in the last half-hour of cooking.

Cool slightly, then drain the beans, reserving the liquid. Return the beans to the pot and mash slightly with a potato masher or the back of a spoon. Heat the olive oil until very hot and pour into the beans, stirring well. Slowly stir in the reserved liquid and the tomato sauce and heat over medium heat for about 15 minutes until heated through and well-blended. Adjust seasonings to taste.

Combine the vinegar and mint leaves in a small cruet. Serve the soup in bowls garnished with croutons, and pass the minted vinegar to sprinkle on the top of the soup.

Slow Cooker Variation: Prepare the beans as directed. Add to the slow cooker along with vegetable stock, onion, garlic and oregano. Cook on high for 6–8 hours or until beans are tender, adding salt in the last hour of cooking.

Cool and drain the beans, then place them in a large stockpot. Follow the remaining steps as directed.

SERVES 4 | *Roasted Corn and Red Pepper Soups*

1 small head garlic

½ teaspoon extra-virgin
olive oil

2 large ears corn

2 tablespoons butter

2 teaspoons red chile powder

3 medium-size red peppers

3 cups smoked-chicken
or vegetable stock

4 carrots, chopped

1 medium-size onion, chopped

4 celery ribs, chopped

2 small seeded and
minced jalapeños

2 cups heavy cream

Salt

Sour cream, for garnish

This is an elegant "day-after" meal when you've barbecued a chicken and grilled corn on the cob. While you have the grill fired up, roast the garlic (page 48), a couple of extra ears of corn (page 85), and the red peppers, then cool and refrigerate to use the next day for the soup.

Preheat grill to medium high. Place garlic bulb on a piece of foil, drizzle with olive oil and wrap tightly. Husk and clean the corn and then place on individual pieces of foil. Make a paste of the butter and chile powder and coat the corn. Wrap tightly in foil. Place garlic and corn on grill, cover it and roast for about 30 minutes. Remove cover and place red peppers on the grill, turning often until skin is blackened all over. Place the peppers in a paper bag to steam. Remove corn and garlic and allow to cool. When cool, squeeze the cloves of garlic into a small bowl and mash. Scrape the kernels from the corn and set aside. Peel the charred skins from the red peppers and remove the stems and seeds. Chop and set aside. (This step can be done a day ahead. Refrigerate the garlic, corn, and peppers until ready for use.)

To make the soups, add the garlic and corn kernels to a medium saucepan. Add half of the chicken stock, carrots, onion, celery, and jalapeño. Bring to a boil over high heat, then reduce heat to low and simmer for 10 minutes. In another saucepan, place the peppers and remaining stock, carrots, onion, celery, and jalapeño. Bring to a boil over high heat, then reduce heat and simmer for 10 minutes.

Remove both soups from heat, and using an immersion blender, puree each soup separately until smooth. You may also use a regular blender. Strain each soup and return to pans. Add one cup of heavy cream to each soup, stir until blended and, over low heat, simmer until thickened, about 5 minutes. Salt to taste.

To serve, use two ladles to simultaneously pour each soup into the bowl, creating a yellow side and a red side. Drop a tablespoon of sour cream into the middle of each bowl and with the tip of a knife, create a marbled effect.

SERVES 8 | ## Caldo de Queso

3 tablespoons extra-virgin olive oil

6 potatoes, peeled and cut into 1-inch cubes

1 large onion, minced

6 green chiles, roasted, peeled, and chopped

8 cups chicken or vegetable stock

½ cup tomato sauce

1 cup half-and-half

½ pound *queso fresco*, crumbled

Salt and pepper

For an interesting twist, try using the smoked-chicken stock in place of the regular chicken or vegetable stock. Queso fresco is a moist, crumbly, and somewhat salty white cheese from Mexico. It's usually available in Mexican markets. If you can't find it, you can substitute a mild feta.

In a Dutch oven or stockpot, heat the olive oil over medium-high heat. Add the potatoes and onion and sauté until the potatoes are slightly browned and the onion is translucent. Stir in the green chiles and sauté 1 minute, then add stock and tomato sauce. Reduce heat to low, cover, and simmer 45 minutes or until potatoes are tender. Stir in the half-and-half and cheese and heat until the cheese is softened. Do not bring to a boil. Add salt and pepper to taste.

SERVES 12 | *Cioppino*

2 tablespoons extra-virgin olive oil

2 cloves garlic, minced

1 medium-size yellow
onion, chopped

1 celery rib, chopped

1 green bell pepper, seeded
and chopped

2 jalapeños, seeded and chopped

½ cup chopped fresh basil or
3 tablespoons dried

2 tablespoons fresh oregano or
2 teaspoons dried

½ cup chopped fresh
Italian parsley

1 teaspoon cracked black pepper

2 teaspoons red chile powder

½ cup dry white wine

¼ cup Worcestershire sauce

¼ cup red wine vinegar

1 tablespoon hot sauce
such as Tabasco

5 cups tomato sauce

1 bay leaf

6 cups seafood stock (page 15)

2 pounds white fish, such
as halibut

1 pound fresh mussels

1 pound peeled and
deveined shrimp

1 pound medium-size sea scallops

A true San Francisco treat; serve this delectable fish stew with warm Italian bread, a green salad, and a California cabernet.

Heat the olive oil over medium heat in a large stockpot or Dutch oven. Add the garlic and onion, stirring until transparent, about 5 minutes. Add the celery, bell pepper, and jalapeños, stirring until soft, about 5 minutes more. Add the basil, oregano, parsley, black pepper, and chile powder, stirring until fragrant. Add the white wine, Worcestershire sauce, red wine vinegar, and hot sauce, stirring until well-blended. Stir in the tomato sauce and bay leaf. Bring to a boil, then reduce heat to low, cover, and simmer for 2 hours.

Remove the bay leaf and add the fish stock to the tomato broth. Increase the heat to medium and bring to a low boil. Cut the fish into 1-inch chunks and scrub the mussels well under running water. Add the fish, mussels, shrimp, and scallops to the broth and cook until the mussels open, the shrimp is pink, and the fish and scallops are translucent. Remove from heat. Discard any mussels that have not opened. Ladle into large serving bowls.

| # Chicken Soup

1 chicken, 2–3 pounds, cut up

2 quarts water

2 cans (14½ ounces each) chopped tomatoes

1 can (4 ounces) tomato paste

3 carrots, sliced

3 celery ribs, tops included, sliced

1 large onion, minced

4 cloves garlic, minced

3 fresh jalapeños, seeded and minced

1 bay leaf

1 tablespoon dried oregano

1 teaspoon ground cumin

1 tablespoon salt

1 teaspoon black pepper

1 cup *acini de pepe* pasta

Sliced avocado, for garnish

Minced green onions, for garnish

Guaranteed to cure the common cold, or at least to make you feel warm and loved.

Clean the chicken and place it in a large stockpot. Cover with water. Bring to a boil over high heat. Skim foam from surface, then reduce heat to low, cover, and simmer for 1 hour. Remove chicken from pot and allow to cool.

Add tomatoes, tomato paste, carrots, celery, onion, garlic, jalapeños, bay leaf, oregano, and cumin to hot stock. Return to boil, then reduce heat, cover, and simmer for 20 minutes. Remove chicken from bones, shred, and add to soup. Add salt and pepper and simmer for another 20 minutes.

Return to a boil, add pasta, and cook until pasta is tender, about 9 minutes. Remove from heat and allow to cool for 5 minutes.

Top each serving with sliced avocado and a sprinkle of minced green onion.

Jalapeño Buffalo Stew

SERVES 8

12 peeled shallots

1 tablespoon extra-virgin olive oil

5 tablespoons vegetable oil

2 pounds buffalo stew meat

½ cup flour

8 jalapeños, stemmed, seeded, and minced

4 carrots, peeled and cut into 2-inch chunks

2 large potatoes, peeled and cut into 2-inch chunks

1 medium-size red onion, diced

1 cup Port wine

4 cups beef stock

2 tablespoons rubbed sage

2 tablespoons dried Mexican oregano

Salt and pepper

Be sure to brown the meat in small batches so that it stays uncrowded in the pan. That way it will brown instead of steam.

Preheat the oven to 350 degrees F. Place the shallots in a small baking pan, drizzle with olive oil, and roast for about 30 minutes or until brown.

Meanwhile, place the buffalo cubes and flour in a zippered plastic bag and shake to coat. Heat the vegetable oil in a Dutch oven or stockpot over high heat. In small batches, sauté the meat in the oil until browned on all sides. Remove and keep warm.

Add the jalapeños, carrots, potatoes, and onion to the pot. Sweat until the onions are transparent and the other vegetables have softened, about 5 minutes. Add the Port and beef stock and bring to a boil, scraping the bottom of the pan to deglaze. Add the sage and oregano. Reduce heat to low, cover, and simmer for 45 minutes. Add the shallots and the buffalo and continue to simmer for another 30 minutes until the buffalo is tender and the vegetables are cooked. Season to taste with salt and pepper.

Slow Cooker Variation: Roast the shallots and brown the meat and vegetables as directed. Deglaze the pan and add the meat, vegetables, Port, stock, sage, oregano, and shallots to the slow cooker. Cover and cook on low for 6-8 hours. Season to taste with salt and pepper.

SERVES 12

Menudo

2 calves' feet

6 quarts water

5 pounds well-cleaned tripe

3 cups *nixtamal*

2 onions, minced

8–10 cloves garlic, minced

6 green chiles, roasted, peeled, and chopped

1 ½ tablespoons salt

1 tablespoon black pepper

2 tablespoons oregano

Minced green onion, for garnish

Lime wedges, for garnish

This is a traditional holiday favorite in the border states. Some claim it cures a New Year's Day hangover. If you can't find tripe or calves' feet in your local grocery, ask at the meat counter. Nixtamal, dried corn kernels soaked in an alkali solution to remove the husks, is available in some grocery freezer sections or in dried form in the Mexican food aisle. If you can't find it, use canned hominy.

Wash the calves' feet thoroughly. Place in a large stockpot and cover with water. Bring to a boil over high heat, then reduce heat to low and simmer for about 1 ½ hours. Remove from heat and cool. Strip the meat from the bones and cut into small chunks. Return the meat to the pot.

Wash the tripe well and cut into 1-inch chunks. Add to the pot. Add the *nixtamal*, onion, garlic, green chile, salt, pepper, and oregano. Add more water if necessary. Bring to a boil over high heat, then reduce heat to low. Cover and simmer for 4–5 hours.

Serve steaming hot in wide bowls sprinkled with green onion and with lime wedges and flour tortillas on the side.

SERVES 8 | Albóndigas

1 ½ pounds lean ground beef

½ pound ground pork

1 teaspoon salt

1 teaspoon black pepper

2 cloves garlic, minced

2 eggs

4 tablespoons masa harina

1 bunch cilantro, minced

1 medium-size onion, finely diced

5 medium-size tomatoes, finely chopped

3 quarts water

1 cup uncooked rice

3 fresh mint leaves, chopped

Another traditional favorite on the border. Masa harina is a corn flour usually available in the baking section or the Mexican food section in grocery stores.

In a large bowl, combine ground beef, ground pork, salt, pepper, garlic, eggs, and masa harina. Use your hands to mix well. Add half of the cilantro, onion, and tomatoes to the meat mixture and mix well, again using your hands. Roll mixture into balls about 1 inch in diameter.

Bring water to a boil. Add remaining half of cilantro, onions, and tomatoes, and then add the rice and mint leaves. Add the meat balls, reduce heat to low, cover, and simmer until rice and meat are cooked, about 45 minutes.

SERVES 8 | *Posole*

2 pounds boneless pork loin

½ cup flour

1 teaspoon salt

1 teaspoon black pepper

2 tablespoons vegetable oil

1 large onion, diced

6 cloves garlic, minced

4 tablespoons red chile powder

2 quarts water

2 cups *nixtamal*

1 teaspoon cumin

1 teaspoon dried oregano

Additional salt

Posole is a traditional New Mexican dish that makes a hearty meal on a cold winter day. If you cook it overnight in a slow cooker, it's also great for breakfast.

Cut the pork loin into 1-inch cubes. Place the flour, salt, and pepper in a zippered plastic bag and shake to mix. Add the pork cubes a few at a time and shake until evenly coated.

Heat the oil over high heat in a large Dutch oven or stockpot. Add the coated pork cubes a few at a time and brown on all sides. Remove as they brown and then add in batches until all of the pork is browned. Add the onion and garlic to the pot and stir until transparent, approximately 5 minutes. Return the pork to the pot and add red chile powder. Stir until coated. Add water, *nixtamal*, cumin, and oregano. If using canned hominy instead of *nixtamal*, add it in the last hour of cooking. Reduce heat to low, cover and simmer for 3 hours or until pork is tender and *nixtamal* has puffed. Add salt to taste in the last 30 minutes of cooking.

Slow Cooker Variation: Brown pork, onion, garlic, and red chile as directed above. Add to slow cooker along with water, *nixtamal*, cumin, and oregano. Cook on high for 8 hours, adding salt to taste in the last hour of cooking.

Serve with warm corn tortillas.

SERVES 6 | *Green Chile Stew* (CHILE VERDE)

2 ½ pounds boneless pork shoulder or loin

2 tablespoons vegetable oil

1 large onion, minced

8 cloves garlic, minced

2 cans (14 ½ ounces each) fire-roasted, diced tomatoes

8 roasted and peeled green chiles, seeded and chopped

2–4 fresh jalapeños, seeded and chopped

6 cups chicken stock

2 cans (4 ounces each) tomato paste

1 tablespoon salt

2 teaspoons black pepper

In Colorado and New Mexico, chile verde is used to smother burritos. You can also serve it as a stew or use it to cover a plate of scrambled eggs and hash browns for breakfast.

Trim the fat from the pork and cut into 1-inch cubes. Heat the oil over high heat in a Dutch oven or stockpot. Add pork and sauté until brown and slightly dry. Add onion and garlic and sauté until onion is translucent, about 5 minutes.

Add tomatoes, green chiles, jalapeños, chicken stock, and tomato paste. Stir to mix thoroughly. Bring to a boil, then reduce heat to low, add salt and pepper, cover, and simmer for 1 hour until meat is tender.

Slow Cooker Variation: Brown the pork in a skillet and add to slow cooker. Sauté the onion and garlic and add to the slow cooker. Using a little water, deglaze the pan and add to the cooker. Stir in tomatoes, chiles, jalapeños, chicken stock, and tomato paste. Add salt and pepper. Cover and cook on high for 4 hours or low for 8 hours.

Serve with warm cornbread or flour tortillas.

SERVES 8 | *Carbonada Criolla*

2 tablespoons vegetable oil

3 pounds boneless pork loin,
cut into 1-inch cubes

1 medium-size onion, diced

6 cloves garlic, minced

1 medium-size green bell
pepper, seeded and chopped

4 tomatoes, chopped

3 cups chicken stock

1 cup white wine

1 teaspoon cilantro, minced

1 teaspoon dried oregano

½ teaspoon crushed
dried red chiles

1 teaspoon salt

¼ teaspoon pepper

3 sweet potatoes, peeled and cut
into 1-inch chunks

1 zucchini, sliced into
½-inch pieces

1 yellow squash, sliced into
½-inch pieces

1 cup fresh or frozen yellow
corn kernels

2 cups dried apricots

You'll find as many versions of this traditional South American meat stew as there are cooks. Almost every version includes sweet potatoes and some form of fruit.

Heat the oil in a Dutch oven and brown the meat in batches, draining well after cooking. Set aside. Add the onion, garlic, bell pepper, and tomatoes to the same pan and cook until soft. Add the stock, wine, cilantro, oregano, crushed red chiles, salt, and pepper, then bring to a boil, stirring and scraping the bottom of the pan. When the mixture reaches a full boil, add the browned pork, reduce heat to simmer, cover, and cook for 30 minutes, stirring occasionally. Add the sweet potatoes and simmer for another 15 minutes, covered, then add the zucchini, yellow squash, corn, and apricots. Cook for another 10 minutes, until the squash is tender.

SERVES 8 | ## Lamb Stew with Frybread

½ cup flour

½ teaspoon salt

½ teaspoon black pepper

2 pounds boneless lamb or mutton, cubed

2 tablespoons vegetable oil

2 quarts water

1 large onion, chopped

3 celery ribs, diced

4 carrots, cut into 1-inch chunks

6 russet potatoes, peeled and cut into ½-inch chunks

1 can (14 ½ ounces) stewed tomatoes

3 yellow squash or zucchinis, sliced

2 tablespoons flour

1 cup water

Frybread (page 33)

Lamb stew is a staple in Native American cultures and makes a hearty dinner, especially when served with traditional frybread.

Combine flour, salt, and pepper in a plastic zipper bag. Add meat in small batches and shake until each piece is completely covered.

Heat the oil in a Dutch oven or stockpot and brown the meat over medium-high heat in small batches. When all of the meat is browned, add it back into the pot.

Use a little water to deglaze the pan, and then add the remaining water and bring to a boil. Reduce heat, cover, and simmer for 30 minutes. Add onion, celery, carrots, and potatoes. Cover and continue to simmer another 30 minutes or until vegetables are tender. Add tomatoes and squash.

Whisk the 2 tablespoons flour into the 1 cup water until flour is completely dissolved. Stir into the stew. Season to taste with salt and pepper. Cover and simmer another 10 minutes or until squash is cooked and stew has thickened.

Slow Cooker Variation: Brown the meat and add to the slow cooker. Deglaze the pan using a little water and add the browned bits to the slow cooker, along with the remaining water. Add the onion, celery, carrots, and potatoes. Cover and cook on low for 6 hours. Add the tomatoes and squash and make a slurry with the flour and water, then stir it into the slow cooker. Cover and cook another hour.

Ladle over frybread (recipe follows) to serve.

MAKES ABOUT 16 | *Frybread*

4 cups all-purpose flour
2 teaspoons baking powder
1 teaspoon salt
1 ½ cups warm water
Canola oil for frying

In addition to serving it with lamb stew, you can top frybread with browned ground beef, beans, lettuce, and cheese for Navajo tacos, or with honey or confectioners' sugar for dessert.

In a large bowl, combine flour, baking powder, and salt. Slowly add enough warm water to form a workable dough. Knead until smooth but still slightly sticky. Cover the bowl with a towel and let the dough rest at room temperature for 30 minutes.

Pull off a piece of dough and roll it into a ball the size of a golf ball. On a lightly floured surface, flatten each ball into a circle about ¼-inch thick.

In a large, deep frying pan, heat 1 inch of canola oil. When it's hot, drop a small piece of dough into the oil. If it rises to the top, the oil is ready. Fry the rounds one at a time, turning once, until golden brown on both sides. Remove from the oil and drain well on paper towels. Keep warm until ready to serve.

Cowboy Beans

2 pounds dried pinto beans

Water to cover beans

1 medium-size onion, minced

4 cloves garlic, minced

6 green chiles, roasted, peeled, and chopped

2 jalapeños, seeded and chopped

1 tablespoon black pepper

2 tablespoons dried oregano

½ pound thick-sliced bacon

Salt

Attend any barbecue in the West and chances are good you'll find some variation of these beans on the menu. Add a can of beer during cooking and they become borracho *(drunk) beans.*

Wash the beans well and sort. Place in a large bowl and cover with cold water. Soak overnight. Drain and discard the soaking water. Place the beans in a large stockpot or Dutch oven. Cover with water by about 2 inches. Bring to a boil over high heat, cover, then reduce heat to low and simmer for an hour until beans are somewhat tender. Salt to taste.

Add onion, garlic, green chiles, jalapeños, pepper, and oregano. Coarsely mince the bacon and stir into pot. Return to a boil, then reduce heat again, cover, and simmer another hour until the beans are soft. Add additional salt if needed.

| SERVES 12 | *Refritos* (REFRIED BEANS) |

2 pounds dry pinto beans

Water to cover

1 tablespoon salt

6 tablespoons lard

1 cup grated Cheddar
or crumbled *queso fresco,*
for garnish

A staple in Mexican cuisine, refritos can be used as a side dish, wrapped in a flour tortilla to make a burrito, used as taco filling or even in tamales. Don't replace the lard with another form of oil—the beans just won't taste the same.

Wash and soak the beans. Place in a large bowl and cover with cold water. Allow to soak 8 hours or overnight until the beans are plump. Drain and discard the soaking water.

Place the beans in a large Dutch oven or stockpot and cover with cold water. Bring to a boil over high heat, then reduce heat to low and cover. Simmer for 1 ½ hours. Add salt and simmer for another hour or until beans are very soft. Remove from heat and strain, reserving the cooking liquid.

Return the beans to the pot and mash with a potato masher or the back of a large spoon. In a small skillet, heat 4 tablespoons of lard until it smokes. Pour into the mashed beans and stir well. Add the cooking liquid and simmer over low heat until the beans are thick, stirring frequently. Heat the remaining two tablespoons of lard until smoking hot and add to beans. Stir well. Remove from heat and garnish with cheese.

| *Gallo Pinto*

1 pound dried black beans

Water to cover beans

1 teaspoon salt

3 tablespoons extra-virgin olive oil

1 cup long-grain white rice

1 medium-size onion, diced

2 cups chicken stock

½ teaspoon salt

½ cup chopped cilantro

3 tablespoons Salsa Lizano or Worcestershire sauce

A traditional Costa Rican dish served for breakfast and lunch. Salsa Lizano is a mildly spicy green vegetable sauce Costa Ricans use on almost everything. Many Latino groceries in the Southwest carry it, or you can order it online.

Wash and sort the black beans. Place in a large bowl and cover with cold water. Soak overnight. Drain, place the beans in a large pot and cover with water to about 2 inches. Bring to a boil over high heat, then reduce heat to low and simmer uncovered for about 1 ½ hours or until soft. Add salt about halfway through cooking time. Remove from heat, set aside.

In a large skillet or Dutch oven, heat 1 tablespoon of the olive oil over medium heat. Stir in the rice and onion. Sauté until the onion is translucent and the rice is coated in oil. Pour in the chicken stock, bring to a boil, add salt, then cover and reduce heat to low. Simmer until the liquid is absorbed and the rice is tender, about 35 minutes. Remove from heat and allow to stand for 5 minutes.

In a large skillet, heat the reamaining 2 tablespoons of olive oil over medium heat. Add several spoonfuls of the beans, along with some of the cooking liquid. Mash the beans slightly and then add the rice and remaining beans and stir to combine. Stir in the cilantro and Salsa Lizano or Worcestershire sauce. Heat through, remove from heat and serve as a main dish or as a side dish with scrambled eggs and warm corn tortillas.

Keeps well in the refrigerator for up to 1 week, and also freezes well for up to 3 months.

Slow Cooker Variation: Rinse and sort the black beans and soak in cold water all day. Drain and add to slow cooker. Cover with water and cook on low overnight. Add salt and cook one more hour while preparing the rice. Finish recipe as directed.

SERVES 4 | *Lobster Shrimp Risotto*

1 lobster tail, about 10 ounces

1 pound large shrimp, about 20 to the pound

2 tablespoons butter

2 tablespoons extra-virgin olive oil

1 cup Arborio or canaroli rice

1 cup dry white wine

1 ½ quarts seafood stock

1 roasted red pepper, peeled, seeded and finely chopped

½ cup freshly grated Parmesan cheese

½ cup julienned fresh basil

Elise Wiggins, executive chef of the award-winning Panzano Restaurant in Denver, graciously shares one of the more popular items on her menu.

Shell and devein the lobster tail and shrimp and use the shells to make the seafood stock (see page 15). Heat the stock to a low simmer.

Slice the lobster tail into chunks and remove the tails from the shrimp. In a large skillet over medium heat, sauté the lobster and shrimp in butter until pink and translucent, about 3–4 minutes. Do not overcook. Remove from the skillet and set aside.

Add the olive oil to the same skillet and heat. Add the rice and stir to coat the grains. Sauté over medium heat for about 5 minutes, stirring constantly to keep the rice from getting brown. Pour in the white wine, turn heat to low, and simmer until wine is absorbed, stirring constantly. Begin to ladle stock into the rice, 1 cup at a time, stirring constantly after each addition. As liquid is absorbed, add more. Repeat until rice is tender and creamy. It should not be crunchy. Add the reserved lobster and shrimp and stir in the roasted red pepper. Stir in the Parmesan cheese and fresh basil. Serve immediately.

| MAKES 4 CUPS | *Creamed Corn* |

12 ears corn
2 cups water
2 tablespoons butter
1 cup whole milk
2 teaspoons flour
Salt and pepper to taste

Make this in the summer when fresh sweet corn is at its peak, and you'll never buy a can again. It's so simple and will keep in the refrigerator for a couple of days, if it lasts that long.

Shuck the corn and scrape off the kernels, reserving the cobs. Place the corn kernels in a medium saucepan with the water and butter. Bring to a boil and then simmer uncovered over medium heat just until the kernels are tender, about 5 minutes.

Over another saucepan, scrape the cobs one more time to extract any last juice. Whisk the flour into ¼ cup of the milk until no lumps remain. Add the remaining milk and the flour mixture to the pan with the corn juice and bring to a boil for one minute, stirring constantly.

Add to the pan with the cooked corn and simmer until thickened. Remove from heat and cool slightly. Using an immersion blender, puree the corn mixture to a half-liquid, half-whole-kernel consistency. Salt and pepper to taste.

Bake

SERVES 4 | *Baked Pork Chops with Peach Whiskey Sauce*

4 boneless pork loin chops, about 1 inch thick

1 cup peach preserves

⅓ cup whiskey

⅓ cup balsamic vinegar

1 tablespoon lemon juice

1 teaspoon ground nutmeg

1 teaspoon ground cinnamon

¼ teaspoon salt

¼ teaspoon freshly ground pepper

1 teaspoon hot sauce, such as Tabasco

When it's too cold to grill but you're craving barbecue, turn on the oven and get these simple pork chops baking in a sweet and spicy sauce. Your taste buds will think it's summer.

Preheat oven to 325 degrees F.

Place the pork chops in a baking pan.

In a small saucepan over medium heat, melt the peach preserves. Stir in the whiskey, vinegar, lemon juice, nutmeg, cinnamon, salt, and pepper. Simmer over low heat, stirring often, until slightly thickened, about 10 minutes. Stir in the hot sauce. Remove from heat.

Pour the sauce over the pork chops, seal the pan with foil, and place in the oven for 45 minutes. Remove the foil and bake for another 15 minutes or until the pork chops are done.

SERVES 12 | Roasted Potato Salad

3 pounds red
potatoes, scrubbed

6 large Roma tomatoes,
seeded and chopped

2 English cucumbers,
peeled and chopped

1 small red onion,
sliced paper-thin

1 cup chopped fresh basil

½ cup chopped fresh parsley

3 tablespoons snipped
fresh chives

1 cup extra-virgin olive oil

⅓ cup red wine vinegar

½ teaspoon salt

½ teaspoon black pepper

2 cloves garlic, pressed

A different twist on traditional potato salad with its mayonnaise and eggs, this is a light and refreshing accompaniment to barbecued chicken or anything from the grill.

Heat oven to 425 degrees F. Place potatoes in a large roasting pan and bake until tender, about 1 hour. Remove from oven and cool. Chop into ½-inch cubes. Place in a large bowl.

Add tomatoes, cucumbers, onion, basil, parsley, and chives to potatoes. Gently toss to mix well.

In a small bowl, whisk together olive oil, vinegar, salt, pepper, and garlic. Pour over salad and toss to coat. Chill for 30 minutes.

SERVES 8	*Potato Pumpkin Gratin*

1 cup all-purpose flour

1 teaspoon salt

1 teaspoon chile powder

1 teaspoon paprika

¼ teaspoon cayenne pepper

¼ teaspoon freshly
ground black pepper

1 ½ pounds fresh pumpkin,
peeled and sliced

1 ½ pounds Yukon Gold
potatoes, peeled and sliced

3 cups heavy cream

1 cup whole milk

1 teaspoon coarse salt

¼ teaspoon freshly
ground black pepper

6 cloves garlic, minced

¾ cup shredded
Gruyère cheese

¾ cup bread crumbs

A hearty fall and winter accompaniment to roast beef or buffalo or a filling vegetarian main dish. You may also use another winter squash, such as Hubbard or butternut, in place of the pumpkin.

Preheat oven to 400 degrees F. Spray a 9" x 13" baking pan with cooking spray. Place the flour, salt, chile powder, paprika, cayenne pepper, and black pepper in a large plastic zipper bag. Shake to mix well. Add the pumpkin slices a few at a time and shake to coat.

Lay half of the pumpkin slices in the prepared pan. Top with half of the potato slices. Repeat layers.

In a large saucepan over medium heat, bring the cream, milk, salt, pepper, and garlic to a simmer. Cook for about 2 minutes without boiling.

Pour the cream mixture over the pumpkin and potatoes. Sprinkle with the cheese and cover tightly with foil. Place in the oven and bake for 20 minutes. Uncover and bake another 20 minutes or until the potatoes and pumpkin are tender.

Sprinkle with bread crumbs and return to oven. Bake another 10 minutes or until bread crumbs are golden brown. Remove from the oven and let stand 10 to 15 minutes.

Scalloped Potatoes and Onions with Goat Cheese

SERVES 12

1 ½ cups heavy cream

1 ½ cups chicken stock

1 cup dry white wine

2 teaspoons minced garlic

1 tablespoon dried thyme

2 teaspoons dried rosemary

2 teaspoons dried sage

8 ounces soft, mild goat cheese

4 pounds russet potatoes, peeled and thinly sliced

1 sweet onion, peeled and thinly sliced

½ teaspoon salt

¼ teaspoon cracked black pepper

Some people aren't fond of the earthy tang of goat cheese. If you're one of them, feel free to substitute an equal amount of ricotta.

Preheat oven to 400 degrees F. Spray a 3-quart glass baking dish with cooking spray.

In a large heavy saucepan over medium heat, bring the cream, chicken stock, white wine, garlic, thyme, rosemary, and sage to a simmer. Whisk in half of the goat cheese until smooth.

Layer the sliced potatoes and onion in the prepared dish. Sprinkle with salt and pepper. Pour the cheese mixture over and cover the dish tightly with foil. Bake for 20 minutes. Uncover and bake until the potatoes are tender, another 45 minutes. Dot the remaining cheese over the potatoes. Return to oven and bake about 5 minutes longer or until the cheese is soft. Remove from oven and cool 15 minutes before serving.

SERVES 4–6

Linguine with Butternut Squash, Walnuts, and Sage Brown Butter Sauce

1 large butternut squash
(3 pounds)

¼ cup butter

Toasted Spicy Rub
(recipe follows)

1 package linguine

1 ½ sticks butter

½ cup fresh sage, cut
into strips

1 cup walnuts, broken
into pieces

Gorgonzola cheese, for garnish

A simple, yet rich and filling fall dish. Serve it as a side or as a main course. You can use whole-wheat linguine for an added nutty taste.

Preheat oven to 400 degrees F. Spray a large baking pan with cooking spray.

Peel the squash with a vegetable peeler, remove seeds, and dice into 1-inch cubes. Arrange in a single layer in the prepared pan. Heat the butter in a skillet until it stops foaming and turns light brown. Remove from heat and pour over the squash, tossing to coat evenly. Sprinkle generously with Toasted Spicy Rub. Bake until fork-tender, about 1 hour. Remove from oven and keep warm.

Prepare linguine according to directions. While pasta is cooking, heat the butter in a large skillet. When it stops foaming and turns light brown, remove from heat and add sage and walnuts. Stir briefly and then stir in the roasted squash, making sure to add any pan drippings.

Add to the cooked and drained linguine, toss to mix and coat the pasta. Sprinkle with crumbled Gorgonzola.

MAKES ¼ CUP	*Toasted Spicy Rub*

I teaspoon fennel seed

I teaspoon coriander seed

I teaspoon cumin seed

I teaspoon green peppercorns

I teaspoon red pepper flakes

I teaspoon chile powder

A versatile rub for sprinkling on roasted meats, potatoes, or winter vegetables.

Place fennel seed, coriander seed, cumin seed, and green peppercorns in a small skillet. Heat over medium heat, stirring and shaking the skillet to prevent the seeds from scorching. After I minute, add the red pepper flakes and chile powder. Continue to shake and stir until the spices are fragrant, about another minute or so. Using a mortar and pestle or spice grinder, grind until fine.

Squash with Cilantro Pesto

SERVES 6

1 large spaghetti squash

1 large zucchini

1 cup Cilantro Pesto
(recipe follows)

½ cup heavy cream

½ cup vegetable stock

Salt

Parmesan cheese, freshly
grated, for garnish

Spaghetti squash, with its strands reminiscent of pasta, is a healthy, gluten-free alternative to traditional spaghetti. If you're a cilantro-hater, use basil or even parsley pesto in its place.

Preheat oven to 350 degrees F. Pierce the skin of the spaghetti squash several times and place on the oven rack. Bake until the skin feels soft, about 1 hour.

While the squash is baking, shred the zucchini into a large bowl.

Remove the spaghetti squash from the oven and allow to cool for 5 minutes. Cut the squash in half lengthwise, scrape out the seeds, and then use a fork to scrape the strands of squash from the shell. Add to the bowl of zucchini and toss to combine.

In a large skillet over medium heat, warm the pesto and stir in the cream and vegetable stock. Add salt to taste. When sauce is warm, add the squash mixture and stir until heated through.

Serve in a large bowl and top with freshly grated Parmesan.

MAKES 1 CUP | *Cilantro Pesto*

¼ pound Parmesan cheese

6 cloves garlic

2 cups fresh cilantro, tightly packed

½ cup piñon nuts or walnuts

¼ cup extra-virgin olive oil

Salt

Excellent on pasta or vegetables or, to make an easy bruschetta, spread on sliced baguettes, top with a strip or two of sun-dried tomato and a small piece of mozzarella, and broil until the cheese melts

Cut the Parmesan into chunks and drop into the bowl of a food processor with the garlic cloves. Process until the cheese is shredded and the garlic is minced. Add the cilantro and nuts. Pulse until the mixture forms a paste. Scrape down the sides of the bowl and then, with the processor running, slowly add olive oil. Process until the pesto is thick. Remove from processor and add salt to taste. Refrigerate for use within a week or freeze for 3 months.

Roasted Garlic

4 bulbs garlic

2 tablespoons extra-virgin olive oil

¼ teaspoon salt

Add to mashed potatoes or spread on French bread. Roasted garlic has a much mellower flavor than fresh.

Preheat oven to 350 degrees F. Cut the top off of each garlic bulb, exposing the tops of the cloves. Place on a sheet of foil. Drizzle the bulbs with olive oil and sprinkle with salt. Seal the foil into an airtight package. Place in the oven and roast for 60 minutes until golden brown and soft. Remove from oven and allow to cool in the foil.

To use, unwrap and squeeze the cloves from the bulb.

| SERVES 6 | *Roasted Root Salad* |

3 parsnips

3 carrots

3 red beets

1 red onion

¼ cup extra-virgin olive oil

1 teaspoon salt

½ teaspoon freshly ground black pepper

1 cup piñon nuts

6 cups mixed salad greens

1 cup Roasted Garlic Vinaigrette (recipe follows)

Cracked black pepper

Roasting root vegetables like beets and parsnips brings out their natural sweetness. If you prefer, use toasted walnuts, hazelnuts, or pecans in place of the piñons.

Preheat oven to 400 degrees F. Trim, scrub, and peel the parsnips, carrots, and beets and peel the onion. Cut all the vegetables into large chunks or wedges. Place in a large roasting pan and drizzle with olive oil. Sprinkle with salt and pepper. Roast in oven for about 1 ½ hours or until vegetables are soft, stirring occasionally. Remove from oven and cool to room temperature.

Place piñon nuts on a baking sheet and roast for ten minutes or until golden brown, stirring frequently to prevent burning. Remove from oven and cool to room temperature.

To assemble salad, place one cup of greens on each plate, then top with vegetable mixture. Sprinkle each plate with toasted piñons and drizzle with dressing. Sprinkle with cracked back pepper. Pass extra dressing at the table.

| *Roasted Garlic Vinaigrette*

3 bulbs roasted garlic

½ cup fresh parsley

⅓ cup balsamic vinegar

1 cup extra-virgin olive oil

½ teaspoon salt

¼ teaspoon black pepper

An unusual and flavorful salad dressing, this vinaigrette also makes a suitable marinade for pork, chicken, fish, or vegetables.

Squeeze the cloves from the garlic bulbs. Add garlic, parsley, and vinegar to the bowl of a food processor. Pulse until well-blended. With the processor running, slowly drizzle in the olive oil. When blended, remove from processor and season with salt and pepper.

SERVES 6–10 | *Piñon Corn Bread Stuffing*

1 pan of corn bread (9" x 9")

1 loaf of white bread

½ cup butter

1 medium-size onion, minced

1 bell pepper, diced

3 celery ribs, sliced

3 fresh jalapeños, seeded and minced

3 eggs

½ cup vegetable stock

1 teaspoon salt

1 tablespoon rubbed sage

1 cup toasted piñon nuts

This is a twist on my grandmother's corn bread stuffing. Bake the corn bread the day before you plan to make the stuffing. If you're roasting a turkey in the oven, you can either stuff the turkey or bake the stuffing in a separate pan. It also works as a side dish for grilled pork chops.

The day before, prepare 1 pan of corn bread according to the directions on a box of cornmeal, omitting the sugar. Let it cool in the pan overnight.

To prepare the stuffing, crumble the corn bread into a large bowl, then shred the white bread and combine it with the corn bread. Set aside.

Preheat oven to 350 degrees F.

In a large skillet, melt the butter and sauté the onion, bell pepper, celery, and jalapeños until they are soft and fragrant, about five minutes. Add the vegetables to the bread mixture and stir to combine. Whisk the eggs together, and then add them to bread mixture, stirring until well-blended. Moisten with warm vegetable stock until the mixture is very wet. Stir in salt and sage, and then add toasted piñon nuts.

Bake in a buttered baking dish at 350 degrees F for 1 hour.

Southwest Corn Bread

1 cup yellow cornmeal

¼ cup sugar

1 teaspoon salt

1 cup flour

3 teaspoons baking powder

1 egg, lightly beaten

1 cup milk

¼ cup vegetable oil

2 cups creamed corn (page 39), or use 1 can (14 ½ ounces)

1 cup cottage cheese

1 cup green chiles, roasted, peeled, seeded, and chopped

1 cup grated Cheddar

This "bread" is so moist and rich that it's almost like a savory pudding. Serve it instead of mashed potatoes with a roast for Sunday dinner.

Preheat oven to 400 degrees F. Spray a 9" x 13" x 2" pan with cooking spray.

In a large bowl, combine the cornmeal, sugar, salt, flour, and baking powder. Make a well in the center and add the egg, milk, and oil. Stir until moistened, leaving lumps. Add creamed corn and cottage cheese, stirring until blended. Avoid the tendency to over mix. Lumps are acceptable.

Pour one half of batter into prepared pan. Cover with green chiles and Cheddar. Top with remaining batter. Bake one hour or until top is golden brown and a knife inserted in the center comes out clean. Remove from oven and cool on a wire rack for ten minutes, then slice into 3-inch squares and remove from pan.

Baked Brown Rice Risotto

SERVES 6

I tablespoon extra-virgin olive oil

I medium-size onion, chopped

I cup short- or medium-grain brown rice

3 cloves garlic, minced

I cup dry white wine

4 cups vegetable stock

½ pound asparagus, trimmed and cut into I-inch pieces

I cup trimmed and cut (I-inch pieces) snow peas

8 ounces fresh spinach

½ cup freshly grated Parmesan cheese

¼ cup chopped fresh chives

2 teaspoons freshly grated lemon zest

Freshly ground pepper

When the first vegetables of spring start showing up in the farmers markets but it's still a little too chilly to fire up the grill, this easy risotto is the answer. The brown rice gives it a full, nutty flavor. And you don't even have to stand over the stove and stir.

Preheat oven to 400 degrees F.

Heat the oil in a Dutch oven over medium heat. Add the onion and cook until translucent, 3–5 minutes. Stir in the rice and garlic. Cook, stirring, I to 2 minutes. Stir in the wine and simmer until absorbed into the rice. Add the vegetable stock and bring to a boil.

Cover the pan and transfer to the oven. Bake until the rice is just tender and the liquid is absorbed, 50 minutes to I hour.

While the rice is baking, steam the asparagus, peas, and spinach until the spinach is wilted and the other vegetables are crisp but tender, about 4 minutes. Remove the rice from the oven and stir in the Parmesan. Fold in the steamed vegetables, chives, and lemon zest.

Sprinkle with ground black pepper and serve immediately.

SERVES 4 | *Honey Mustard Baked Chicken*

1 frying chicken, cut into pieces

½ teaspoon salt

½ teaspoon pepper

¼ cup extra-virgin olive oil

⅓ cup honey

⅓ cup Dijon mustard

2 tablespoons fresh lemon juice

An easy-to-prepare middle-of-the-week dinner, especially good with steamed veggies and warm sourdough bread. If you can, learn to cut up a whole chicken and avoid those plastic-wrapped pieces you find in the meat case. It's less expensive and doesn't take that much extra time.

Preheat oven to 350 degrees F.

Sprinkle the chicken on all sides with salt and pepper. Place in a single layer in a 9" x 13" baking pan. Drizzle with olive oil.

Combine the honey, mustard, and lemon juice. Pour over the chicken. Bake uncovered for 1 hour, turning the chicken pieces once and basting with the pan juices at least twice.

Remove from oven, place chicken on a warm platter and drizzle with the remaining pan juices.

| ## Turkey Mole

½ cup blanched almonds

4 tablespoons sesame seeds

1 tablespoon extra-virgin olive oil

1 ripe plantain (skin should be almost black), sliced

2 tablespoons ancho chile powder

2 tablespoons pasilla chile powder

2 tablespoons chipotle powder

2 teaspoons ground cinnamon

1 teaspoon salt

4 corn tortillas, shredded

1 small onion, diced

6 cloves garlic

4 ripe tomatoes, peeled and seeded

6 cups chicken stock

1 tablet Mexican chocolate, grated

1 turkey breast, about 3–5 pounds

The origins of mole are somewhat murky, and in Mexico you'll find many different regional variations, but this recipe will give you a spicy, savory sauce that freezes well and can also be used for enchiladas or as a sauce to smother burritos.

Preheat oven to 350 degrees F. Spread the blanched almonds on a baking sheet and place in the oven. Roast until browned, stirring occasionally. Set aside. Reduce the oven temperature to 325 degrees F.

In a small sauté pan, heat the sesame seeds, stirring several times until golden brown. Set aside. In the same pan, heat the olive oil and add the slices of plantain. Sauté until soft.

In the bowl of a blender or food processor combine the almonds, sesame seeds, plantain, three kinds of chile powder, cinnamon, salt, shredded tortillas, onion, garlic, and tomatoes. Process until pureed. Add a little of the chicken stock and continue to process to make a smooth paste.

In a large, heavy saucepan, stir together the paste and remaining chicken stock, cooking over medium heat. Add the chocolate and stir until melted. Continue to cook until the sauce is thickened. Taste and adjust seasonings, if necessary.

Place the turkey breast in a roasting pan. Cover with the prepared sauce and bake, covered, until the internal temperature reaches 160 degrees F, about 1 ½–2 hours. Reserve any extra sauce to pass with the turkey. Remove the turkey from the oven and allow to sit for about 10 minutes before slicing.

SERVES 6 | *Stuffed Peppers*

6 red, green, or yellow bell peppers, or a mixture

3 cups water

1 pound lean ground beef

¼ cup finely minced onion

2 cloves finely minced garlic

½ teaspoon salt

½ teaspoon pepper

3 tablespoons chile powder

1 cup cooked rice

½ cup fresh or frozen corn kernels

1 can (14 ½ ounces) tomatoes

3 tablespoons water

½ cup grated Cheddar

Comfort food at its finest. Use red and yellow peppers to add color and interest.

Preheat oven to 350 degrees F. Remove the tops and the seeds from the bell peppers. Bring 3 cups of water to a boil in a medium saucepan. Using tongs, plunge the peppers into the water one at a time and hold for about 10 seconds to blanch. Remove to a wire rack and drain.

In a large skillet over medium heat, brown the ground beef. Stir in the onion and garlic and continue to cook until the onion is softened. Add the salt, pepper, and chile powder and stir until the beef is coated. Stir in the rice, corn kernels, and tomatoes. Cook for about 5 minutes until the mixture is thickened.

Place the peppers in a pan large enough to hold them and stuff each one with the meat mixture. Add three tablespoons of water to the bottom of the pan, seal with foil, and place in the oven. Bake for 45 minutes. Remove foil, top the peppers with Cheddar and bake for another 15 minutes or until the Cheddar is melted.

Slow Cooker Variation: Prepare the peppers and the meat mixture as directed. Stuff the peppers and arrange in a slow cooker. Add 3 tablespoons of water to the cooker, cover and cook on low for 8 hours. Remove cover and sprinkle the peppers with the Cheddar. Cover and cook for another hour.

SERVES 8 | *Smoked Sausage Strata*

1 loaf (16 ounces) crusty whole-grain French bread

1 red onion, diced

6 cloves garlic, minced

2 tablespoons extra-virgin olive oil

1 pound smoked sausage, sliced into 1-inch chunks

1 package (10 ounces) thawed frozen spinach

1 cup julienned sun-dried tomatoes

1 cup shredded Swiss cheese

8 eggs, slightly beaten

3 cups half-and-half

½ teaspoon pepper

This is a good make-ahead dish if you have a few minutes in the morning. Assemble and refrigerate and then when you get home at the end of the day, it's ready to go into the oven. Make a green salad, open a bottle of wine, and you have dinner.

Slice the bread into 1-inch cubes and allow to dry several hours on a wire rack. Alternatively, arrange the cubes in a single layer on a baking sheet and place in a 300-degree F oven for 15–20 minutes, or until dry but not toasted.

In a large skillet over medium heat, sauté the onion and garlic in olive oil until fragrant, about 5 minutes. Add the sliced smoked sausage and sauté until the sausage is browned and the onions and garlic are soft, stirring frequently.

Squeeze the excess liquid from the spinach. Add to the skillet and stir, cooking just until the spinach is warmed. Add the sun-dried tomatoes and cook a few minutes longer, stirring frequently. Remove from heat and allow to cool slightly.

Spray a 9" x 13" pan with cooking spray. Arrange half of the bread cubes in the bottom of the pan. Spread the sausage mixture over the top. Top with the cheese, then with the remaining bread cubes.

In a medium bowl, whisk the eggs and then add half-and-half, stirring to combine well. Add pepper. Pour the egg mixture over the contents of the pan. Cover the pan with plastic wrap and place a plate on top to keep the contents submerged in the egg mixture. Allow to sit at room temperature for about 30 minutes.

Preheat the oven to 350 degrees F.

Uncover the pan and bake for one hour or until the top is lightly puffed and brown. Remove from oven and allow to sit at room temperature for 10 minutes before slicing and serving.

SERVES 4 | *Lamb and Rice Pitas*

---

1 ½ pounds boneless lamb shoulder, cubed into half-inch pieces

2 medium-size onions, quartered

2 tablespoons extra-virgin olive oil

1 teaspoon cinnamon

¼ cup pine nuts

2 tablespoons tomato paste

Salt and black pepper

2 cups long-grain rice

2 ½ cups boiling water

6 pitas

Chopped cucumber, for garnish

Chopped tomato, for garnish

Plain yogurt, for garnish

A fun make-it-yourself dinner.

Preheat the oven to 350 degrees F.

In a Dutch oven over medium heat, sauté the lamb and onions in the olive oil until the meat is tender. Stir in the cinnamon and nuts and sauté until the nuts are lightly browned. Stir in the tomato paste and season to taste with salt and pepper. Spread in an even layer over the bottom of the Dutch oven. Spread the rice over the top. Pour in the boiling water. Cover and place in the oven.

Bake until the rice is tender, about one hour. Remove from the oven, uncover, and place a serving platter over the Dutch oven. Invert onto the plate. Warm the pita rounds. Cut them in half.

Place the platter, a basket of pitas, and dishes of cucumbers, tomatoes, and yogurt on the table. Allow each guest to stuff the pita halves with a serving of the lamb-and-rice mixture, and then garnish as desired.

SERVES 8 | *Chorizo Green Chile French Toast*

½ pound Mexican chorizo

8 eggs

2 cups milk

½ teaspoon salt

½ teaspoon pepper

12 slices (½-inch each) dried French bread

1 stick softened butter

4 green chiles, roasted, peeled and seeded

1 cup grated Cheddar

1 cup grated Monterey Jack cheese

If you want to impress your brunch guests and make them think you've been in the kitchen since early morning, this is the way to do it. Assemble this casserole the night before, sleep in, and then pop it into the oven while the coffee brews. Set the table, slice some fruit, and you're ready to go.

Brown the chorizo in a skillet over medium-high heat. Drain on paper towels.

In a medium bowl, whisk together the eggs, milk, salt, and pepper.

Spray a 9" x 13" baking pan with cooking spray. Coat both sides of the bread with the softened butter. Place six slices in the prepared pan, squeezing to fit, if necessary. Pour half of the egg mixture over the bread to coat. Cover the bread layer with green chiles. Add the chorizo and then cover with half of the Cheddar and Monterrey Jack. Cover with the remaining bread.

Pour the remaining egg mixture over all and top with the remaining cheeses. Tightly cover the pan with foil and refrigerate overnight.

Remove the pan from the refrigerator and allow to sit at room temperature for 30 minutes. Preheat the oven to 350 degrees F. Place the uncovered pan in the oven and bake for one hour or until the surface is puffy and lightly browned and the cheese is melted.

Remove from oven and allow to sit at room temperature for 10 minutes before serving.

SERVES 6	*Bourbon Baked Beans*

1 pound dried navy beans

Water to cover beans

2 teaspoons dry mustard

1 teaspoon black pepper

½ teaspoon ground ginger

1 ½ tablespoons cider vinegar

1 ½ cups strong coffee

½ cup maple syrup

2 tablespoons molasses

1 medium-size onion, minced

¼ pound salt pork

¼ cup bourbon

A traditional barbecue accompaniment, best baked in a traditional bean pot. If you don't have one, use any deep casserole.

Wash and sort the beans. Place in a large bowl and cover with cold water. Allow to soak overnight. Drain the beans and place them in a stockpot. Cover with water and, over high heat, bring to a boil. Reduce heat to low and simmer uncovered for about 30 minutes until beans are slightly softened.

Preheat oven to 275 degrees F. Drain the beans, reserving the cooking liquid. Place them in a 2-quart bean pot. In a medium bowl, combine mustard, pepper, ginger, and vinegar. Stir in coffee, maple syrup, molasses, and 1 ½ cups of the reserved cooking liquid. Pour over the beans to cover, adding more cooking liquid if needed. Stir in the onion. Score the fatty side of the salt pork and place it rind-side down on top of the beans. Cover, place in the oven, and bake the beans for 6–7 hours.

Remove the beans from the oven and stir in the bourbon. If the beans seem too dry, add more of the cooking liquid. Return to oven and bake another hour. Remove cover and bake another 30 minutes until the top is nicely crusted. Remove from oven and serve immediately.

SERVES 4 | *Stuffed Winter Squash*

4 medium-size acorn squash, halved and seeded

2 teaspoons extra-virgin olive oil

Salt

Freshly ground black pepper

½ cup water

½ pound rigatoni

1 tablespoon extra-virgin olive oil

½ cup chopped onion

2 tablespoons finely minced garlic

2 teaspoons salt

2 ½ cups peeled and chopped fresh tomatoes, including juice

¼ cup chopped fresh basil

½ cup vegetable stock

½ teaspoon black pepper

1 pound Italian sausage, casing removed and cut into ½-inch pieces

1 cup sliced red onion

½ pound mozzarella, shredded

This is a winter favorite around our house because it satisfies both the pasta and the vegetable lovers. This also freezes well. After baking, wrap each serving in foil and freeze. To serve, thaw and reheat in the oven until the stuffing is bubbling.

Preheat the oven to 350 degrees F. Drizzle the squash with the 2 teaspoons of olive oil and season with salt and pepper. Place in a baking pan cut-side-up and add ½ cup water to bottom of the pan. Tightly cover the pan with foil and bake until the squash is tender, about 1 hour. Remove from the oven.

While the squash is baking, prepare the stuffing:

Cook the rigatoni according to package directions. When done, remove from heat and toss with a small amount of olive oil. Set aside.

Heat 1 tablespoon olive oil in a large skillet over medium-high heat. Add the onion and garlic and sauté until the onion is translucent. Add the salt, tomatoes, and basil and cook for a few minutes until the tomatoes are soft. Stir in the stock and black pepper and simmer for another 3 minutes. Remove from heat and set aside.

In a large skillet over medium heat, brown the sausage and onion. Combine the pasta, tomato sauce, and sausage. Add the cheese, mixing well.

Drain any remaining water from the baking pan. Spoon the stuffing into the squash halves. Return to the oven and bake for 10 minutes or until the stuffing is heated through.

Slow Cook

| ## Beer-braised Corned Beef

1 corned beef brisket,
3–5 pounds

Fresh water for soaking

2 cups carrots

2 cups blanched and peeled
boiling onions

1 pound red potatoes,
cut into wedges

1 bay leaf

2 tablespoons Dijon mustard

2 tablespoons molasses

1 bottle (12 ounces) stout beer

1 small head cabbage,
cut into wedges

It might come as a shock to some people, but Tucson is known as the home of the country's best corned beef. Soaking the brisket in cold water will remove the excess salt without taking anything away from the flavor.

In the refrigerator, soak the brisket in cold water for 12 hours to remove the excess salt from the curing process, changing the water several times.

In the bottom of a slow cooker, place the carrots, onions, and potatoes. Place the soaked brisket on top, fat side up. Add the bay leaf.

In a small bowl, whisk together the mustard and molasses, and then add the beer, stirring to blend. Pour over the contents of the slow cooker. Cover and cook on low for 8 hours. Place the cabbage wedges on top of the brisket, cover, and cook for another hour.

To serve, slice the brisket against the grain. Serve with a loaf of warm rye bread, some grainy mustard, and plenty of stout.

SERVES 8 | ## Ratatouille Frittata

I small eggplant with peel, cut into ½-inch pieces

I cup finely chopped onion

I medium-size red bell pepper, chopped

I yellow bell pepper, chopped

3 large zucchini sliced ¼-inch thick, with peel

3 cloves garlic, finely minced

¾ pound cherry tomatoes

½ teaspoon salt

¼ teaspoon pepper

½ teaspoon dried oregano

½ teaspoon dried tarragon

½ teaspoon dried thyme

½ teaspoon fennel seeds

I bay leaf

12 eggs

¼ cup half-and-half

Salt and pepper

½ cup freshly grated Parmesan or Pecorino Romano cheese

A frittata makes a simple dinner or brunch dish. Use any leftover ratatouille as a garnish for roasted meat or as a topping for French bread. Place on a slice of bread, sprinkle with cheese, and broil until bubbling.

Place eggplant, onion, bell peppers, zucchini, garlic, cherry tomatoes, salt, pepper, oregano, tarragon, thyme, fennel seeds, and bay leaf into a slow cooker. Stir, cover, and cook on low for 8 to 9 hours or high for 4 to 4 ½ hours. (This step may be done one day in advance. Refrigerate the ratatouille until ready for use.)

Strain the excess liquid from the ratatouille and spread a thick layer in a 12-inch ovenproof skillet. In a large bowl, whisk the eggs until completely blended. Stir in the half-and-half and season with salt and pepper. Pour the egg mixture over the ratatouille. Cook over medium heat for 3 or 4 minutes, mixing gently with a spatula, until the eggs begin to set. Sprinkle the cheese over the top.

Heat the broiler and place the skillet about 4-6 inches from the heat. Broil until the eggs are cooked and the cheese is melted. Remove from broiler and allow to stand another 5 minutes.

Cut into wedges and serve with toasted French bread and a green salad.

SERVES 8 | ## *Calabacitas con Chorizo*

I pound Mexican chorizo

2 tablespoons extra-virgin
olive oil

I small onion, sliced thin

4 cloves garlic, minced

4 zucchini, sliced

4 yellow squash, sliced

2 cups fresh or frozen
corn kernels

4 green chiles, roasted, peeled,
and chopped

4 large tomatoes, peeled,
seeded, and chopped

2 tablespoons red chile powder

2 teaspoons fresh or
½ teaspoon dried oregano

I teaspoon salt

½ teaspoon pepper

Grated Monterey Jack or
Cheddar cheese, for garnish

Calabacitas is a traditional dish of the Southwest. The addition of chorizo, a Mexican bulk sausage, gives it enough body to become a main course.

In a large skillet over medium-high heat, brown the chorizo. Drain the grease and place the browned sausage into a slow cooker. Wipe the skillet with a paper towel, then heat the olive oil. Sauté the onion and garlic just until soft. Add to the slow cooker. Add zucchini, yellow squash, corn, chiles, and tomatoes, and stir well. Stir in the chile powder, oregano, salt, and pepper.

Cook on low for about 6 hours. Before serving, garnish with grated cheese.

Chile Relleno Casserole

12 corn tortillas

3 cups cooked,
shredded chicken

1 ½ pounds green chiles,
roasted, peeled, and seeded

3 cups grated Cheddar

1 ½ cups grated Monterey
Jack cheese

4 eggs, lightly beaten

1 ½ cups milk

1 teaspoon salt

½ teaspoon pepper

Salsa, for garnish

Sour cream, for garnish

This cheesy delight can derail anyone who is watching fat intake, so cut down on the serving size. Instead of a main course, turn it into an appetizer by cutting into squares instead of wedges.

Spray the bottom and sides of the slow cooker with cooking spray. Tear four of the tortillas into large chunks and cover the bottom of the slow cooker. Cover the tortillas with one cup of the chicken. Open the green chiles and layer one-third of them on top of the chicken. Top with one cup of the Cheddar and ½ cup of the Monterey Jack. Repeat, beginning with the tortillas and ending with the cheese. For the final layer, add the remaining tortillas, chicken, and green chiles, but set aside the cheese.

Whisk together the eggs, milk, salt, and pepper. Pour over the layers in the slow cooker. Top with the remaining cheese. Cover and cook on low for 4 hours.

To serve, allow to cool for 10 minutes. Turn out of the slow cooker onto a large plate and cut into wedges. Serve with salsa and sour cream.

SERVES 4

Lemon Chicken

1 teaspoon dried oregano

½ teaspoon salt

¼ teaspoon ground black pepper

4 skinless, boneless chicken breast halves

2 tablespoons extra-virgin olive oil

½ cup chicken stock

3 tablespoons fresh lemon juice

2 cloves garlic, minced

1 teaspoon chopped fresh parsley

Serve with steamed rice and a green salad.

In a small bowl, combine the oregano, salt, and pepper. Rub the mixture into the chicken breasts. Heat the olive oil in a skillet over medium heat. Brown chicken for 3 to 5 minutes on each side. Place chicken in a slow cooker.

In the same skillet, mix the chicken stock, lemon juice, and garlic. Bring the mixture to a boil and deglaze the pan, scraping up the browned bits. Pour over the chicken in the slow cooker.

Cover and cook on low for 6 hours. Add the parsley 15 minutes before the end of the cooking time.

SERVES 6 | ## Southwest Chicken Breasts

6 boneless, skinless
chicken breasts

½ cup shredded Cheddar

¼ cup minced green
bell pepper

¼ cup minced red bell pepper

¼ cup minced cilantro

¼ cup seeded and
diced tomatoes

1 teaspoon chile powder

½ teaspoon ground cumin

Salt

1 cup red chile sauce
(see page 75)

If you don't want to make your own chile sauce, you can use canned enchilada sauce.

Place each chicken breast between 2 slices of wax paper and gently pound with a meat mallet until ¼-inch thick.

In a medium bowl, mix the shredded Cheddar, green pepper, red pepper, cilantro, and tomatoes. Stir in the chile powder, cumin, and a pinch of salt.

Place one-sixth of the cheese mixture on each chicken breast. Roll and secure with 2–3 toothpicks. Place the rolled chicken breasts in the slow cooker. Cover with 1 cup of the chile sauce. Cover and cook on low for 6 hours, or on high for 3.

Serve with rice and beans.

SERVES 4–6 | ## Chicken Enchiladas

4 boneless, skinless chicken breasts

Salt and pepper

2 cups red chile sauce (recipe follows)

½ cup vegetable oil

1 dozen corn tortillas

¾ cup sliced green onions

1 cup sliced black olives

1 cup grated Cheddar

1 cup crumbled *queso fresco*

You can cook the chicken in advance, refrigerate for up to two days, and then make the enchiladas.

Place the chicken breasts in the slow cooker. Season with salt and pepper. Cover with ¾ cup of the chile sauce. Reserve the remaining chile sauce. Cover and cook on low for 6 hours. Remove from slow cooker and shred the chicken.

Preheat oven to 350 degrees F. Spray a 9" x 13" pan with cooking spray.

In a small skillet, heat the vegetable oil over medium heat. In a small saucepan, heat the remaining chile sauce over low heat just until warm.

One at a time, dip the corn tortillas into the hot oil until softened, about 5 seconds, and then into the chile sauce. Place in the prepared pan and top with a small amount of chicken, onions, olives, and Cheddar. Roll and place seam-side-down in the pan. Repeat with the remaining tortillas, arranging the filled rolls to fit in the pan.

Pour the remaining red chile sauce over the top of the enchiladas, then sprinkle with the Cheddar and the *queso fresco*.

Place in the oven for 25 minutes or until the cheese is melted. Remove from oven and serve immediately, garnishing with the remaining green onions and olives.

MAKES 2 CUPS	*Red Chile Sauce*

8–10 dried red New Mexico chiles, seeds and stems removed

2 cups water

2 tablespoons vegetable oil

2 tablespoons flour

Salt

This is easy and tastes much better than canned chile or enchilada sauce. Make a big batch and freeze the extra so you always have it on hand for covering tamales, burritos, or scrambled eggs. If you use chiles from a ristra, make sure they haven't been sprayed with preservative. Cookbook author Deborah Madison suggests adding a few drops of vinegar to smooth out the flavor, if needed.

Preheat oven to 250 degrees F. Place the chiles on a baking sheet and toast for about 10 minutes, turning to keep from burning. Remove from oven, cool, and crumble into a medium saucepan. Add water and bring to a boil.

Remove from heat and allow to cool slightly. Add the mixture to a blender or food processor and process until the sauce is smooth.

In a deep skillet, heat the oil over medium-high heat. Add the flour and stir until it begins to brown slightly. Stir in the chile sauce and cook until thickened. Add salt to taste.

SERVES 8 | ## Turkey Chili

2 pounds ground turkey

1 cup red chile powder

1 large onion, minced

2 green bell peppers, finely chopped

3 celery ribs, finely chopped

8 cloves garlic, minced

1 teaspoon cumin

2 teaspoons salt

1 teaspoon ground black pepper

2 cans (14 ½ ounces each) drained and rinsed black beans

2 cans (14 ½ ounces each) chopped tomatoes

This is a low-fat alternative to regular chili. Because the turkey is less flavorful than beef, be sure to add plenty of seasonings. Serve with hot corn bread or fresh flour tortillas.

Brown the turkey in a large skillet over high heat. As it browns, add chile powder. Place the cooked turkey in a slow cooker. In the same skillet over medium heat, sauté the onion, peppers, celery, and garlic until fragrant and translucent. Add to the slow cooker. Stir in the cumin, salt, pepper, black beans, and tomatoes, adding a little water if necessary to bring liquid to the level of the other ingredients. Cook on high for 3–4 hours, or on low for 6–8.

SERVES 4–6

Turkey Picadillo Tacos

I pound ground turkey

2 tablespoons extra-virgin olive oil

I medium-size yellow onion, minced

2 cloves garlic, minced

½ cup tomato sauce

2 fresh tomatoes, peeled, seeded and chopped

½ cup chopped green olives

½ cup raisins

½ teaspoon dried oregano

I teaspoon salt

½ teaspoon pepper

12 corn tortillas

Vegetable oil for frying

Sliced green onions, for garnish

Sour cream, for garnish

Chopped lettuce, for garnish

Traditional picadillo is a hash common in the Caribbean and Latin America. Different regions use different ingredients, but the base is almost always ground beef. This version with turkey is a little more lean, but feel free to use ground beef if you prefer.

In a large skillet over medium-high heat, brown the turkey. Place in a slow cooker. Add olive oil to the skillet and sauté the onion until soft, about 5 minutes. Add the garlic and sauté for another minute. Add the onion and garlic to the slow cooker. Add tomato sauce, tomatoes, olives, and raisins to the slow cooker and stir well to combine. Stir in oregano, salt, and pepper.

Cook on low for 5 hours. If the picadillo is too soupy, remove from the cooker and heat in a skillet until fairly dry.

Make taco shells by dipping each corn tortilla in hot oil and shaping it until crisp. Drain on paper towels. Fill with picadillo and garnish with sliced green onions, sour cream and lettuce. Serve immediately.

SERVES 4–6 | *Carne Adovada*

½ teaspoon ground cumin

½ teaspoon dried oregano

½ teaspoon ground cayenne pepper

½ teaspoon garlic salt

½ teaspoon salt

½ teaspoon pepper

4 boneless pork loin chops, 1 inch thick

½ cup chile powder

1 cup water

My sister Theresa is a great cook and came up with this easy and delicious version of carne adovada. If you have any leftovers, scramble together with eggs for breakfast.

In a small bowl, combine the cumin, oregano, cayenne pepper, garlic salt, salt, and pepper. Sprinkle over the pork chops. Place in a slow cooker. Add the chile powder and water. Cover and cook on low for 6–8 hours. Remove from cooker and shred the meat with two forks.

Pour the sauce from the slow cooker into a small saucepan and reduce over medium-high heat until thickened. Pour over the shredded meat.

Serve with warm flour tortillas and pico de gallo (page 113).

Jalapeño Pulled Pork

SERVES 6

4 pounds pork shoulder, bone-in

I teaspoon whole cumin seeds

I teaspoon whole fennel seeds

I teaspoon whole coriander seeds

I tablespoon chile powder

I tablespoon paprika

2 red onions, sliced

6 jalapeños, seeded, stemmed, and sliced

2 cups water

2 cups Spicy Chipotle Barbecue Sauce (page 90) or your favorite

Pulled pork is usually considered a Southern dish, but the addition of jalapeños adds a Western zing.

Remove the pork shoulder from the refrigerator. In a small skillet over medium heat, toast the cumin, fennel, and coriander seeds until fragrant. Grind together with the chile powder and paprika. Sprinkle over the surface of the pork.

Add half of the onion slices and jalapeños to the bottom of the slow cooker. Place the seasoned pork on top and cover with the remaining onions and jalapeños. Pour in the water, cover, and cook on low for 8–10 hours.

Remove the meat from the cooker and shred, removing the bones. Return to the cooker, stir in the barbecue sauce, cover, and cook for an additional 2 hours, adding a small amount of water if needed to keep the mixture moist.

Serve with whole grain rolls, sliced onions, and dill pickles.

SERVES 6 | Tamale Casserole

I pound ground pork

½ pound lean ground beef

2 tablespoons extra-virgin olive oil

I large onion, chopped

3 cloves garlic, minced

I can (28 ounces) whole tomatoes

I cup yellow cornmeal

2 cups fresh or frozen yellow corn kernels

2 eggs

I teaspoon salt

½ teaspoon black pepper

¼ cup New Mexico chile powder

Put this in the slow cooker in the morning, put together a green salad when you get home, and dinner is served.

Spray the inside of the slow cooker with cooking spray.

In a large skillet over medium-high heat, brown the pork and beef. Drain and set aside.

Add the olive oil to the same skillet and sauté the onion and garlic until soft. Puree the tomatoes in a food processor. Stir into the onion and garlic. Slowly add the cornmeal, stirring constantly to prevent lumping. Remove from heat. Add the meat and corn kernels to the mixture in the skillet. Beat the eggs lightly and stir into the mixture. Blend in the salt, pepper, and chile powder.

Pour the mixture into the slow cooker. Cover and cook on low for 6 to 8 hours.

SERVES 8

Beef in Red Wine Sauce

3 pounds beef chuck, cut into
1-inch cubes

½ cup flour

1 teaspoon salt

½ teaspoon pepper

3 tablespoons extra-virgin
olive oil

1 cup dry red wine

1 can (28 ounces) undrained
Italian tomatoes

1 bay leaf

1 teaspoon salt

½ teaspoon pepper

1 teaspoon dried thyme

2 strips (2-inch) orange peel

1 pound boiling onions

2 pounds unpeeled small
red potatoes

Serve over a bed of white rice or buttered noodles.

Dry the beef with a paper towel. Combine the flour, salt, and pepper in a zippered plastic bag and add the beef cubes in small batches, shaking to coat.

Heat the oil in a large skillet over medium-high heat. Brown the beef in small batches and transfer to the slow cooker. When all of the beef has browned, use ½ cup of the wine to deglaze the pan, scraping up the browned bits. Pour into the slow cooker along with the remaining wine and Italian tomatoes. Add the bay leaf, salt, pepper, thyme, and orange peel. Cook on low for 6 hours.

Parboil and peel the onions. Add the onions and red potatoes to the slow cooker and cook for another 1 ½ hours until the potatoes are tender. Discard the bay leaf and orange peel.

SERVES 6 | *Asian Beef*

2 pounds beef top round steak

2 large onions, cut into wedges

½ cup unsweetened
pineapple juice

½ cup beef stock

5 tablespoons red wine vinegar

3 cloves garlic, minced

¾ teaspoon salt

I teaspoon paprika

½ teaspoon ground
black pepper

I teaspoon red chile flakes

I green bell pepper, cut
into I-inch squares

I red bell pepper, cut
into I-inch squares

3 tablespoons brown sugar

I ½ tablespoons cornstarch

2 tablespoons light soy sauce

½ fresh pineapple, cut
into I-inch chunks

White or brown rice

An easy slow-cooker version of sweet and sour beef.

Trim the fat from the beef and slice into thin strips diagonally across the grain. Place in the slow cooker. Add the onions, pineapple juice, beef stock, 3 tablespoons of the vinegar, garlic, salt, paprika, black pepper, and red chile flakes. Mix well.

Cover and cook on low 6 hours or until the beef is just tender. Increase the heat to high. Stir in the green and red peppers and the brown sugar. In a small bowl, whisk together the cornstarch, soy sauce, and remaining 2 tablespoons vinegar. Stir into the cooker, blending well.

Cover and cook on high 45 minutes, stirring occasionally, until the sauce thickens.

Just before serving, stir in the pineapple chunks. Serve over steamed white or brown rice.

Barbecue / Smoke

Roasted Corn on the Cob

SERVES 8

8 ears of corn, husks attached
1 stick butter, softened
1 tablespoon chile powder
½ teaspoon garlic salt
1 teaspoon ground cumin

Slow roasting caramelizes the sugar in the corn, and the presoak in cold water keeps the ears moist during the cooking process.

Pull the husks back on the corn, but leave in place. Remove the silk and trim the end of each cob. Pull the husks back into place and place the corn in a large pot of ice water. Soak for 1 hour.

Heat the grill to low, about 300 degrees F. Move the coals to one side. If using a gas grill, follow the manufacturer's instructions for indirect cooking.

Remove the corn from the ice water, pull the husks back and dry with a paper towel.

In a small bowl, combine the softened butter, chile powder, garlic salt, and cumin. Coat each ear of corn with the mixture and pull the husk back into place, making sure that the entire ear is covered. Remove a small strip of husk and tie it around the small end of the ear to keep the husk in place.

Place the corn on the grill away from the coals, cover the grill, and roast for 45 minutes, turning occasionally. Serve immediately.

SERVES 8	*Roasted Sweet Potatoes*

6 large sweet potatoes or yams

Cold water to cover

3 tablespoons extra-virgin olive oil

3 tablespoons lime juice

3 tablespoons Dijon mustard

1 tablespoon chile powder

1 clove garlic, crushed

½ teaspoon salt

½ teaspoon black pepper

½ teaspoon cayenne pepper

If heating up the grill isn't appealing, you may roast the sweet potatoes in the oven, but you'll lose the distinct smoky flavor.

Heat the grill to medium-high, about 450 degrees F. Peel the sweet potatoes and cut into large chunks. Place in a bowl and cover with cold water.

In a small bowl, whisk together olive oil, lime juice, mustard, chile powder, garlic, salt, pepper, and cayenne pepper. Drain the water from the sweet potatoes and dry with a paper towel. Return to the bowl and add the marinade, tossing to coat. Place the potatoes in a grilling basket and set on a grill over medium-high indirect heat. Cover and roast until the potatoes are tender, about 45 minutes. Turn or stir as needed during the roasting time.

Do-it-yourself Chipotles

MAKES ½ POUND

5 pounds red jalapeños

Hickory, pecan, or other hardwood chips or chunks

If you like to garden and you find yourself with a bumper crop of jalapeños, leave them on the plant until they turn red, then harvest and make your own chipotles. You can also use the green peppers.

Wash the jalapeños and discard any that have blemishes or soft spots. Remove the stems and make a small slit in the side of each one.

Soak the wood in water for at least 1 hour. Prepare the smoker and bring the heat to 200 degrees F.

Place the peppers in a single layer on the top rack in the smoker, farthest away from the heat. If the peppers are too small for the rack, cut a piece of wire mesh to fit and place it on the rack underneath the peppers. Cover and allow to smoke for 3–5 hours or until the peppers are shriveled and pliable. Stir about once an hour and make sure that the temperature and smoke stay constant.

The smoked peppers will still contain a small amount of moisture. To dry completely, use a food dehydrator or place on the rack in an oven at very low temperature until the peppers are brown and hard.

To reconstitute for use in sauces, soak in hot water for approximately 30 minutes. Use as-is to make chipotles in adobo sauce (page 91). You can also grind them with a mortar and pestle or in a food processor to make chipotle powder. Wear a painter's mask to keep the dust from your nose.

Store in tightly sealed zippered plastic bags for up to 6 months.

SERVES 6 | *Beer Can Chicken*

2 large chickens, whole

1 cup balsamic vinegar

¾ cup extra-virgin olive oil

¼ cup Dijon mustard

¼ cup honey

4 garlic cloves, minced

3 shallots, minced

1 ½ teaspoons salt

2 ½ teaspoons black pepper

2 tablespoons sugar

1 tablespoon paprika

1 tablespoon red chile powder

1 teaspoon ground
cayenne pepper

1 tablespoon garlic powder

2 tablespoons dried onions

1 tablespoon dried mustard

2 cans beer

½ cup dry white wine

This was a big barbecue trend a few years ago, but the fact is that the beer keeps the chicken moist and tender. If you resisted the fad the last time around, try it now. You'll never again barbecue chicken without a can of beer (in the chicken, that is). You may need an assistant to help remove the chickens from the grill without spilling the beer.

Remove neck and giblets from the chickens and discard. Rinse the chickens well and pat dry.

In a large bowl, whisk together the balsamic vinegar, olive oil, mustard, honey, garlic, shallots, ½ teaspoon salt and ½ teaspoon black pepper. Place each chicken in a large zippered plastic bag and pour half of marinade over each. Seal the bags tightly and place in the refrigerator overnight. Turn the chickens occasionally to make sure they marinate evenly. The chickens can marinate for up to 24 hours.

In a small bowl, thoroughly mix the sugar, paprika, chile powder, cayenne pepper, garlic powder, dried onions, mustard, 2 teaspoons black pepper and 1 teaspoon salt.

Remove the chickens from the marinade and sprinkle inside and out with the rub, making sure that each is completely coated.

Heat the grill to low heat (about 250 degrees F) and pile the coals around the sides. If using a gas grill, follow the manufacturer's directions for indirect grilling. Make a drip pan out of foil, set it in the middle of the grill underneath the rack, and add a small amount of water. When the grill has reached the proper temperature, open the cans of beer and discard (or drink) half. Set the cans on the grill over the drip pan. Carefully place the chicken cavities over the cans of beer, making sure that they remain upright. Cover the grill and adjust the vents to hold the temperature.

Pour the white wine into a clean spray bottle. Once every hour, spray the chickens with the white wine and rotate them 90 degrees, making sure that they continue to stay upright on top of the cans. Add more coals to the grill as needed to keep the temperature constant. Cook the chickens for 4 hours or until an instant-read thermometer inserted into the deepest part of the thigh reaches 170 degrees F. The temperature will continue to rise when they are removed from the heat.

Carefully remove the chickens from the grill by lifting them off the cans of beer and placing them breast-side-down on a large rimmed baking sheet. Allow to rest for ten minutes. Discard the beer. Pour any collected juices from inside the chickens and from the baking sheet into a bowl and turn the chickens over. Remove the legs and thighs whole and slice the remaining meat from the bone. Reserve the carcasses for making stock (page 13). Arrange on a platter and pour the reserved juices over. Serve with Spicy Chipotle Barbecue Sauce (page 90).

| MAKES 1 QUART | *Spicy Chipotle Barbecue Sauce* |

3 cups ketchup

⅔ cup brown sugar

½ cup water

½ cup white wine vinegar

2 tablespoons mustard powder

2 tablespoons red chile powder

½ teaspoon ground cayenne pepper

1 tablespoon black pepper

1 teaspoon salt

4 cloves garlic, finely minced

¼ cup onion, finely minced

3 chipotles in adobo sauce, finely minced (recipe follows, or use canned)

3 tablespoons adobo sauce

This is a versatile barbecue sauce for any kind of meat. If you want to reduce the spiciness, reduce the amount of adobo sauce.

In a heavy saucepan over low heat, combine ketchup, brown sugar, water, white wine vinegar, mustard powder, chile powder, cayenne pepper, black pepper, salt, garlic, onion, chipotles, and adobo sauce. Stir well and allow to slowly simmer for one hour. Serve with barbecued chicken, brisket, ribs, or pork.

Keep in a tightly sealed container in the refrigerator for up to 1 month, or freeze for up to 3 months.

Chipotles in Adobo Sauce

12 chipotle peppers
(see page 87)

4 cups water

½ cup diced onion

⅓ cup cider vinegar

¼ cup ketchup

3 cloves garlic, minced

¼ teaspoon cumin

¼ teaspoon oregano

¼ teaspoon salt

Combine the chipotles, water, onion, vinegar, ketchup, garlic, cumin, oregano, and salt in a heavy saucepan. Simmer over low heat for 1–2 hours until the chiles are soft and the liquid has been reduced to about 1 cup.

Slow Cooker Variation: Place all of the ingredients in a slow cooker. Cover and cook on low for at least 8 hours. Uncover and cook on high for 1 hour or until sauce is reduced.

To make a sauce for marinades or as a table condiment, puree in a blender until smooth. Refrigerate tightly covered for up to 6 weeks or freeze for up to 3 months.

| MAKES 3 PIZZAS (12-INCH) | *Jerk Chicken Pizza* |

3 tablespoons dark rum

2 tablespoons water

¼ cup cider vinegar

2 bunches green onions, trimmed and sliced

6 garlic cloves, minced

I habañero, seeded and minced

I tablespoon dried thyme

I tablespoon ground allspice

I tablespoon ground ginger

I tablespoon ground cinnamon

2 teaspoons ground nutmeg

I teaspoon salt

2 teaspoons ground black pepper

2 teaspoons dark brown sugar

2 tablespoons extra-virgin olive oil

I cup ketchup

3 tablespoons soy sauce

2 roasting chickens, 3- to 3 ½-pound

½ cup fresh lime juice

I tablespoon active dry yeast

I ½ cups warm water

3 ½ cups flour

I tablespoon extra-virgin olive oil

Marinate and barbecue two chickens. Use one for the pizza and save one for dinner the next day. Just wrap it in foil, refrigerate, and heat at 350 degrees F for 30 minutes. While this has many steps, because you do it in stages and get two meals, it isn't all that time-intensive.

Combine rum, water, vinegar, green onions, garlic, habañero, thyme, allspice, ginger, cinnamon, nutmeg, salt, pepper, and brown sugar in a food processor. Process until smooth. With the processor running, pour in the olive oil and pulse until blended.

Remove 2 tablespoons of the seasoning mixture to a small bowl. Stir in the ketchup and soy sauce. Cover and refrigerate.

Place the chickens in a large dish. Pour lime juice over them, then coat with the remaining seasoning mixture. Cover and refrigerate overnight, turning several times.

Preheat the grill to 300 degrees F. Move the coals to one side and place a foil drip pan under the cooking grate. Add a small amount of water. If using a gas grill, follow manufacturer's instructions for indirect grilling. Place the chickens on the grill and roast for I ½–2 hours until an instant-read thermometer inserted in the thickest part of the thigh reads 170 degrees F. Remove the chickens from the grill and allow to rest for 15 minutes. (This step can be done a day in advance. Wrap the chickens in foil and refrigerate.)

2 tablespoons cornmeal

1 red onion, thinly sliced and separated into rings

3 green peppers, thinly sliced in rings

3 cups grated mozzarella

Make the pizza dough. Sprinkle the yeast over the warm water and allow to stand for about five minutes. Place the flour in a large bowl and make a well in the center. Add the yeast and the olive oil. Mix by hand until the flour is incorporated and a dough forms.

Sprinkle a little flour on the work surface. Shape the dough into a ball and knead by hand for about 5 minutes until the dough no longer sticks to your hands. Wipe a little olive oil into the bowl, shape the dough into a ball and place in the bowl. Rub a little olive oil on the surface, cover with a dry towel and place in a warm, draft-free location. Allow to rise until doubled in size, about 1–2 hours.

To make the pizza, shred the cooked chicken and set aside. Preheat the oven to 500 degrees F.

Lightly oil a baking sheet or pizza pan and sprinkle with some cornmeal to prevent the pizza from sticking. If you're using a pizza stone, preheat it in the oven and then sprinkle a wooden pizza peel with the cornmeal.

Punch down the pizza dough in the bowl and move to a flour-covered work surface. Cut into three equal pieces. Roll and stretch the first piece into a 12-inch round. Place on the prepared pan or pizza peel.

Spread several tablespoons of the reserved jerk sauce on the surface of the dough. Cover with shredded chicken, then add a layer of onion rings and pepper rings. Sprinkle with cheese. Place the pizza in the oven and cook for about 10 minutes. Bake until the cheese is melted and the dough is golden brown. Remove from oven, slice, and serve. Repeat with remaining dough and toppings.

SERVES 6 | *Barbecued Southwestern Turkey*

1 fresh turkey, 12–14 pounds

½ cup butter, softened

2 tablespoons red chile powder

1 tablespoon ground cumin

1 clove garlic, finely minced

½ teaspoon black pepper

1 teaspoon salt

1 orange, cut into eighths, peel on

1 apple, cored and sliced

1 onion, quartered

2 cups fresh orange juice

1 cup white wine

If you're lucky enough to live in a warm climate, a barbecued turkey at Thanksgiving is a delicious change from the traditional method. If you have to do this in the oven, it works just as well. It just doesn't have the smoky taste. Serve with Piñon Cornbread Stuffing (page 53).

Remove the turkey from the refrigerator and allow to sit at room temperature for 30 minutes. Heat the grill to low (about 300 degrees F) and push the coals to one side. Prepare a drip pan. If using a gas grill, follow the manufacturer's directions for indirect heat grilling.

Remove the giblets from the turkey and discard, or save for making gravy. Rinse the bird and pat it dry. Work the softened butter underneath the turkey skin. Make a rub by mixing the chile powder, cumin, garlic, pepper, and salt in a small bowl. Sprinkle over the entire turkey. Place the orange, apple, and onion pieces in the body cavity. Sprinkle with salt, tuck the wing ends under, and secure the legs.

Place the turkey on the grill over the drip pan and cover the grill. Baste periodically with a mixture of the orange juice and white wine, and roast until an instant-read thermometer reads 170 degrees F, approximately 3–4 hours. Remove from the grill and allow to stand for about 30 minutes before carving.

Country-style Ribs

SERVES 4–6

4–5 pounds country-style
pork ribs

3 tablespoons chile powder

1 tablespoon cocoa powder

1 tablespoon paprika

1 teaspoon cayenne pepper

1 teaspoon ground cumin

½ teaspoon salt

1 teaspoon pepper

½ cup dry white wine

½ cup apple juice

Jalapeño Lime Barbecue
Sauce (page 96)

Country-style ribs are meatier and fatter than spare ribs, which makes them good for a long, slow cook over low heat.

Place the ribs in a single layer on a large rimmed baking sheet. In a small bowl, combine the chile powder, cocoa powder, paprika, cayenne pepper, cumin, salt, and pepper. Mix well. Sprinkle over the ribs and coat evenly.

Preheat the grill to 225 degrees F. Move the coals to one side and place a drip pan under the cooking grate. Add a small amount of water to the drip pan. If using a gas grill, follow manufacturer's instructions for indirect grilling.

Place the ribs on the grill, cover, and cook until tender and falling off the bone, about 3 hours. Spray periodically with a mixture of white wine and apple juice.

Remove from grill and brush with Jalapeño Lime Barbecue Sauce (recipe follows). Pass extra sauce on the side.

Jalapeño Lime Barbecue Sauce

MAKES 1 ½ CUPS

½ cup ketchup

¼ cup balsamic vinegar

2–4 jalapeños, seeded and
finely minced

¼ cup dark molasses

Juice of 1 lime

1 can (5 ½ ounces) vegetable
juice, such as V-8

2 cloves garlic, pressed

This is one of those "whatever's in the kitchen" recipes that came about when neighbors dropped by at dinnertime. Serve with country-style spare ribs, burgers, or anything else from the grill. Control the heat by increasing or reducing the number of jalapeños.

Mix ketchup, vinegar, jalapeños, molasses, lime juice, vegetable juice, and garlic in a small sauce pan. Heat over medium and then lower heat so that the sauce barely simmers for 20 minutes or until thickened.

Smoked Pork Loin

SERVES 6

½ cup soy sauce

¼ cup balsamic vinegar

¼ cup apple juice

2 tablespoons sesame oil

1 tablespoon powdered ginger

2 cloves crushed garlic

3-pound boneless pork loin

½ pound mesquite chips,
for smoking

Do this for a special summer dinner, or make it a day ahead and serve cold for brunch. Leftovers keep for several days and, along with some mustard and hard rolls, make delicious sandwiches.

Whisk together soy sauce, vinegar, apple juice, sesame oil, ginger, and garlic. Place pork loin in a plastic zipper bag and pour marinade over. Allow to marinate in the refrigerator overnight or 8 hours.

Remove the pork loin from the refrigerator and allow to sit at room temperature for 30 minutes. Soak the mesquite chips in water and then prepare the smoker according to manufacturer's directions. Add the pork loin and smoke at low heat for 3 hours or until the internal temperature reads 160 degrees F, adding mesquite chips as necessary. Remove pork from smoker and allow to sit at room temperature for 15 minutes. Slice and serve warm or cold.

SERVES 8 | *Cheesy Cedar-plank Salmon*

1 Alaskan salmon
fillet, 3 pounds

½ teaspoon garlic salt

½ teaspoon black pepper

Juice of one lemon

½ cup mayonnaise

⅓ cup Gorgonzola
cheese, crumbled

⅓ cup Parmesan cheese,
freshly grated

⅓ cup mozzarella, grated

Many high-end grocers and butchers now carry cedar planks for cooking fish. You can pay top dollar there, or you can visit your local lumberyard for a piece of ½ x 8-inch untreated cedar in a length that will hold the fillet and fit inside your grill. Be sure to use wild salmon and not farmed. Wild salmon is healthier for you and better for the environment.

Soak the cedar plank in water to cover for one hour.

Place the salmon skin-side-down on a large non-reactive tray and sprinkle with garlic salt, pepper, and lemon juice. Let sit for 30 minutes.

Preheat the grill to low heat (about 225 degrees F) and move the coals to one side. If using a gas grill, follow manufacturer's instructions for indirect heat.

In a medium bowl, combine the mayonnaise, Gorgonzola, Parmesan, and mozzarella until well-blended. Remove the plank from the water. Place the salmon on the plank, skin-side-down, and then cover the fish with a thick layer of the cheese mixture.

Place the plank on the grill away from the coals. Cover and adjust the vents to maintain low heat. Grill for about 45 minutes until the cheese is melted and bubbly and the salmon is translucent in the center, rotating the plank 180 degrees once during the cooking process. Cooking time may vary depending on the thickness of the salmon.

Smoked Rocky Mountain Trout

SERVES 4 AS A MAIN COURSE,
OR 8–10 AS AN APPETIZER

⅓ cup kosher salt

1 quart water

4 whole trout, cleaned and heads removed

Alder or oak chips

Serve this as an appetizer or light lunch right out of the smoker. If you have any left (not likely, but you can dream), mix it with cream cheese and a little onion for a crowd-pleasing dip.

Dissolve the salt in the water. Place the fish in a large glass baking dish and pour the salt water over to cover. Allow to sit at room temperature for one hour.

In the meantime, heat the smoker or grill to about 200 degrees F according to the manufacturer's directions. Soak a few handfuls of alder or oak chips in a container of water.

Drain and rinse the fish and then place in the smoker for 3 hours, adding wood chips as needed. Remove the bones and skin and serve immediately with whole grain crackers or French bread, or refrigerate tightly wrapped for up to one week.

SERVES 12 | ## Barbecued Beef Brisket

1 large beef brisket,
about 10 pounds

⅓ cup Dijon mustard

2 tablespoons cider vinegar

1 tablespoon brown sugar

2 teaspoons Worcestershire sauce

1 teaspoon hot sauce,
such as Tabasco

2 tablespoons sugar

2 tablespoons brown sugar

2 tablespoons paprika

2 tablespoons garlic salt

1 tablespoon chile powder

1 ½ teaspoon ground
black pepper

½ teaspoon ground cumin

½ teaspoon ground
cayenne pepper

½ teaspoon Italian
seasoning blend

4 cups chicken broth

½ cup cider vinegar

½ cup Worcestershire sauce

6 garlic cloves, finely minced

½ cup grated onion

1 bay leaf

1 teaspoon salt

1 teaspoon pepper

Spicy Chipotle Barbeque Sauce
(page 90)

Because this takes so long, you can make it a day or two in advance, wrap in foil, and refrigerate. Reheat in a 325-degree oven for about one hour.

Remove the brisket from the refrigerator and place on a large, rimmed baking sheet or tray.

Make the slather by whisking together the Dijon mustard, cider vinegar, brown sugar, Worcestershire sauce, and hot sauce in a small bowl. Rub over the brisket to cover completely.

Make the rub by combining the sugar, brown sugar, paprika, garlic salt, chile powder, black pepper, cumin, cayenne pepper, and Italian seasoning in a small bowl. Sprinkle over the entire brisket and allow the brisket to sit at room temperature for at least an hour.

Make the mop by bringing the chicken broth, vinegar, Worcestershire sauce, garlic, onion, bay leaf, salt, and pepper to a boil in a medium saucepan over high heat. Reduce heat and simmer for 20 minutes. Cool and strain.

Heat the grill to 225 degrees F. Push the coals to one side and place a drip pan under the grate. Fill with water. If using a gas grill, follow the manufacturer's directions for indirect cooking.

Place the brisket on the grate fat-side-up and away from the heat. Cover the grill and cook 4 hours, adding more coals as needed and moistening with the mop every hour. After 4 hours, flip the brisket over and continue to cook another 6 hours, adding coals as needed and mopping every hour. Turn the brisket 2 more times during the cooking. The brisket is done when the temperature in the thickest part reaches 180 degrees F.

Remove from the grill and allow to stand for 15 minutes. Slice against the grain and serve with Spicy Chipotle Barbecue Sauce.

SERVES 6

Smoky Prime Rib

1 bone-in prime rib roast, 5–6 pounds

6 garlic cloves

¼ cup fresh rosemary

¼ cup fresh basil

2 teaspoons kosher salt

2 teaspoons black pepper

3 tablespoons Dijon mustard

3 tablespoons extra-virgin olive oil

1 cup mesquite chips

Garlic Blue Cheese Horseradish Sauce (page 103)

The most important detail when roasting a prime rib is to avoid overcooking. The meat will continue to cook after leaving the heat, so pay close attention to the internal temperature and let it rest after it comes out of the oven.

Remove the roast from the refrigerator and let stand at room temperature for 45 minutes.

Prepare the rub. Combine the garlic, rosemary, basil, salt, pepper, and mustard in the bowl of a food processor. Process until smooth. With the processor running, gradually pour in the olive oil until emulsified. Trim the fat from the beef and cover the surface of the roast with the rub.

In the meantime, heat the smoker to low, about 200–225 degrees F. Prepare a drip pan to go under the meat and add 1 inch of water. Soak mesquite chips in water.

Place the roast in the smoker and add a handful of soaked mesquite chips to the coals. Cover and allow to cook at low heat for 1 hour. After an hour, turn the roast and add more mesquite chips. Maintain the temperature in the smoker and allow the meat to cook for 30 minutes per pound or until it reaches an internal temperature of 110 degrees F for medium-rare.

Just before removing the meat from the smoker, preheat the oven to 400 degrees F. Remove the roast from the smoker and place on a rack in a large roasting pan. Turn off the oven and place the roast inside for approximately 15–20 minutes or until it reaches 125 degrees F with an instant-read thermometer. Remove the roast from the oven, tent with foil and allow to sit for 20 minutes.

Slice and serve with Garlic Blue Cheese Horseradish Sauce (recipe follows).

MAKES ¾ CUP | ## Garlic Blue Cheese Horseradish Sauce

¼ cup heavy cream

3 tablespoons prepared horseradish

¼ cup sour cream

2 cloves garlic, minced

1 teaspoon dry mustard

red chile powder

¼ teaspoon ground white pepper

¼ cup crumbled blue cheese

If you have any left after dinner, use it as a dressing on roast beef sandwiches.

Combine the cream, horseradish, sour cream, garlic, mustard, chile powder, and white pepper in the bowl of a food processor. Process until smooth. Remove from the processor and stir in crumbled blue cheese. Serve immediately over roast beef. Refrigerate in a tightly sealed container and use within 1 week.

SERVES 6–8 | *Barbecued Roast Beef*

1 eye of round roast,
3 ½–5 pounds

¼ cup sweet vermouth

¼ cup extra-virgin olive oil

½ cup brewed strong
black coffee

3 teaspoons ground fennel seed

3 cloves garlic, pressed

½ teaspoon onion powder

1 teaspoon salt

½ teaspoon black pepper

Don't overcook! The internal temperature of the roast will continue to rise during the resting period.

Place the roast in a large plastic zippered bag. Whisk together the vermouth, olive oil, coffee, fennel seed, garlic, onion powder, salt, and pepper. Pour over roast. Seal and refrigerate for 3 hours, turning occasionally. Remove from the refrigerator and allow to sit at room temperature for 30 minutes.

Preheat the grill to low, about 225 degrees F. Move the coals to one side and place a drip pan in the middle. If using gas, follow manufacturer's directions for indirect grilling. Remove the roast from the bag and reserve the marinade. Place the roast on the grill and cover. Roast for 2 ½ to 3 ½ hours, brushing with marinade occasionally. Internal temperature should reach 120 degrees F for medium rare. Remove from grill and allow to stand for 20 minutes before slicing.

SERVES 6 | *Peppercorn Buffalo Roast with Dijon Sauce*

1 buffalo sirloin tip roast, 3-pound

2 tablespoons Dijon mustard

1 tablespoon lemon juice

2 cloves garlic, pressed

2 tablespoons coarsely ground black pepper

1 teaspoon salt

½ teaspoon dried oregano

8 ounces sour cream

1 tablespoon Dijon mustard

1 teaspoon fresh lemon juice

1 teaspoon prepared horseradish

Buffalo is available at many high-end grocers and butcher counters, or directly from producers (see Sources, page 142). Because it is so lean, it requires a great deal of care in the cooking. Don't overcook and be sure to let it rest when it comes off the heat so the natural juices can disperse through the meat.

Bring the roast to room temperature.

In a small bowl, make a paste of the mustard, lemon juice, garlic, pepper, salt, and oregano. Rub the paste over the surface of the roast. Place in a plastic zipper bag and marinate overnight.

Remove the roast from the refrigerator and allow to sit at room temperature for 1 hour. Preheat the grill to medium (about 325 degrees F) and move the coals to one side. Place a drip pan under the cooking grate and add about an inch of water. If using a gas grill, follow the manufacturer's directions for indirect cooking. Place the roast on the cooking grate, cover the grill, and roast for 2 hours or until the roast reaches 120 degrees F for medium rare. Remove from the grill and allow to stand at room temperature for 20 minutes.

Meanwhile, in a small bowl, combine the sour cream, mustard, lemon juice, and horseradish.

To serve, slice the roast and garnish with the sauce.

Spicy Southwestern Leg of Lamb

SERVES 6

6 cloves garlic

6 fresh jalapeños, seeded

½ cup tequila

4 teaspoons Dijon mustard

1 teaspoon salt

2 teaspoons black pepper

1 leg of lamb, bone
in, 5–6 pounds

Cherry-Mint Sauce
(recipe follows)

The jalapeños add subtle spice to the meat without making it too hot. This is another cut of meat that should never be overcooked.

Puree the garlic, jalapeños, tequila, mustard, salt, and pepper in the bowl of a food processor. Place the lamb in a large glass baking dish and coat with the marinade. Cover and marinate 8 hours, turning occasionally.

Preheat the grill to 225 degrees F. Move the coals to one side. If using a gas grill, follow the manufacturer's instructions for indirect grilling. Place the lamb on the grill away from the coals and cover. Roast until the temperature reads 135 degrees F for medium rare. Remove from the grill and allow to stand for 15 minutes to allow juices to move into meat. Carve and serve with Cherry-Mint Sauce on the side.

Cherry-Mint Sauce

MAKES 1 ½ CUPS

1 jar (8 ounce) cherry preserves

¼ cup mint jelly

¼ cup prepared horseradish

½ teaspoon mustard powder

Works well with lamb or even bison.

Combine the cherry preserves, mint jelly, horseradish, and mustard in a small saucepan. Melt over low heat, stirring to combine. Remove from heat and chill before serving.

Braise

Chorizo-stuffed Artichokes

SERVES 4

3 quarts cold water

4 lemons

4 large globe artichokes

½ cup Mexican chorizo

¼ cup onion, minced

½ cup dry bread crumbs

½ cup grated Monterey Jack cheese

½ teaspoon salt

½ cup water

Jalapeño Garlic Aioli (page 110)

Mexican chorizo is fresh and made from pork, garlic, chile powder, and other spices, depending on the maker. It is vastly different from Spanish chorizo, the cured sausage flavored with smoky Spanish paprika.

In a bowl large enough to hold all four artichokes, squeeze the juice of three lemons into the cold water. Slice remaining lemon in half and set aside.

Prepare the artichokes for stuffing: Cut the stem end so that the artichoke sits flat. Remove the tough outer leaves. Slice about one inch from the top of each artichoke, exposing the purple-tipped inner leaves. Rub the cut surfaces with the reserved lemon to keep from turning brown. Remove the inner leaves in one clump, using a twisting motion. Using a small spoon, scrape out the fuzzy center, exposing the heart. Sprinkle the heart with lemon juice. Trim the tips from any remaining leaves, rubbing with lemon. Place each prepared artichoke in the bowl of cold water.

In a medium skillet, brown the chorizo over medium heat. Remove from pan and drain. Wipe the excess grease from the pan. Add the minced onion to the same pan and cook until translucent, about 5 minutes. Combine the onions, chorizo, bread crumbs, cheese, and salt in a medium bowl.

Remove the artichokes from the water and drain upside-down for a minute or two. Turn right-side-up and place a little less than ¼ of the stuffing in the center of each. Place remaining stuffing inside each of the outer leaves so that the entire artichoke is filled.

Preheat oven to 375 degrees F. In a heavy Dutch oven or braising pan, bring ½ cup of water to a simmer. Place the stuffed artichokes into the pan. Place a layer of parchment over the artichokes and then cover with a tight-fitting lid or foil. Place in the oven and braise for 90 minutes.

Remove from the oven. Place each artichoke on a serving plate and drizzle with Jalapeño Garlic Aioli (recipe follows).

MAKES I CUP | ## Jalapeño Garlic Aioli

---

1 bulb roasted garlic (page 48)
2 egg yolks at room temperature
1 jalapeño, seeded and minced
1 teaspoon Dijon mustard
1 tablespoon fresh lemon juice
1 cup extra-virgin olive oil
½ teaspoon salt
Pinch of fresh pepper

Excellent on fish tacos or cold roasted pork loin. To avoid contaminating the egg yolks with salmonella, break the egg into the palm of your hand and allow the white to drain through your fingers.

Squeeze the cloves from the bulb of garlic. Place the egg yolks, jalapeño, garlic, mustard and lemon juice in the bowl of a food processor. Process until the yolks are light and lemony and the mixture is well blended. With the processor running, add the olive oil in a light stream. Don't add too much too quickly or it won't emulsify. When the mixture is blended, remove from processor and stir in the salt and pepper.

Refrigerate and use within 1 day.

SERVES 8 | *Angel Hair with Peperonata*

2 pounds sweet Italian peppers

¼ cup extra-virgin olive oil

1 medium-size sweet onion, thickly sliced

6 Roma tomatoes, seeded, peeled, and chopped

½ teaspoon salt

½ teaspoon black pepper

1 teaspoon crushed red pepper flakes

½ cup dry white wine

1 package (8 ounces) angel hair pasta

½ cup freshly grated Parmesan cheese

½ cup fresh basil, torn into pieces

In the late summer when the garden is full of peppers, tomatoes, and basil, invite some friends over to make jars of peperonata, and then celebrate your accomplishment with some pasta and a glass of wine on the patio. The sauce can be made in multiples depending on the bounty of your harvest, and then either frozen or canned.

Remove the stems and seeds from the sweet peppers and cut them into 1-inch chunks.

In a large braising pan or skillet with a heavy lid, heat the olive oil over medium-high heat. Add the onion slices and sauté until the onions are softened but not browned, about 8 minutes. Stir frequently. Add the peppers and tomatoes. Reduce heat to low and add the salt, pepper, crushed red pepper flakes, and white wine. Bring to a simmer and then cover. Braise over low heat for 45–50 minutes, making sure that the liquid is barely simmering and that the vegetables are not sticking. If the liquid cooks down too much, add more wine.

Just before the peperonata is finished, cook the angel hair according to the package directions.

Place several spoonfuls of the peperonata into a large warmed pasta bowl. Add the drained angel hair and then top with the remaining peperonata. Toss to combine. Top with Parmesan cheese and fresh basil.

SERVES 8 | *Yucatan Pork Roast* (PUERCO PIBIL)

2 tablespoons cumin seeds

4 large garlic cloves

1 tablespoon salt

1 tablespoon dried oregano

2 dried serrano chiles, crumbled into flakes

¼ cup *achiote* paste

1 tablespoon orange juice

Juice of 1 lime

3–4 large banana leaves, fresh or frozen

1 whole pork shoulder, bone-in, about 8 pounds

Juice of 3 oranges

Juice of 2 limes

2 dozen corn tortillas

Pico de Gallo (recipe follows)

If you're lucky enough to live in a place where bananas grow, just pick some leaves and heat them over a gas flame until they're pliable. If you can't pick your own, find them frozen at Asian or Mexican supermarkets. In any case, the banana leaf adds an important earthy flavor, so while you can use foil for a wrap in a pinch, it's worth it to find the banana leaves. Achiote paste is made from ground annatto seeds and can be found in Mexican groceries.

Place the cumin in a small skillet over high heat. Shake until the cumin is lightly toasted and fragrant. Remove from the skillet and set aside. Finely mince the garlic until it resembles a paste. Knead in the salt. Place the garlic-salt paste in a small bowl and stir in the toasted cumin, oregano, chiles, *achiote* paste and the orange and lime juice. The mixture should be thick.

Thaw the banana leaves. If you're using fresh, heat over an open flame until they're slightly darkened and pliable. Trim the ribs from the center of each leaf and set aside.

Rub the paste over the entire pork shoulder, coating all surfaces. Place the roast on a banana leaf and fold it neatly around the meat. Place seam-side-down on another leaf, perpendicular to the first leaf, and wrap again. Repeat until the roast is completely covered by about 3 layers of leaves. Use the leaf ribs or cotton kitchen string to tie the leaves in place. Set on a rack in a large baking pan and refrigerate for 24 hours.

Remove the pork from the refrigerator and bring to room temperature.

Heat the oven to 300 degrees F.

Pour the orange and lime juices into the bottom of the pan. Cover tightly with foil and place in the oven. Braise for 3 hours. Remove foil and carefully turn the roast. Add more juice or a little water to the pan, if needed. Seal again with foil and continue to braise for another 2 to 3 hours.

To serve, remove the roast from the roasting pan to a large platter. Cut the string and tear open the banana leaves. Shred the meat with a fork and place in the middle of the table. Pass around warm corn tortillas and pico de gallo.

MAKES 3 CUPS | *Pico de Gallo*

---

1 small onion, finely chopped

2–3 jalapeños, seeded and chopped

1 cup finely chopped cilantro

1 pound tomatoes, seeded and chopped

1 avocado, chopped

Juice of 1 lime

Salt

Also great for tacos or with a big bowl of chips.

Combine the onion, jalapeños, cilantro, tomatoes, and avocado in a medium bowl. Sprinkle with lime juice and salt to taste. Stir and serve immediately.

SERVES 6–8 | *Carnitas*

1 bone-in pork shoulder,
5 pounds

2 tablespoons vegetable oil

2 teaspoons cumin

2 teaspoons oregano

1 large onion, sliced

6 cloves garlic, minced

1 teaspoon salt

½ teaspoon pepper

1 quart beef broth

Tortillas

Pico de gallo (page 113)

Guacamole, for garnish

Refritos (page 35)

Carnitas are a weekend favorite at many Mexican restaurants. The long braise makes the meat tender and succulent while the quick roast to finish gives it a contrasting crunch.

Wipe the pork shoulder dry with a paper towel. In a large Dutch oven, heat the oil over medium-high heat. Add the pork and brown on all sides. Reduce heat to medium and add the cumin, oregano, onion, and garlic. Stir until the onion softens. Add the salt and pepper and cover with beef broth. Cover with a tight-fitting lid, place in the oven at 300 degrees F, and allow to simmer gently for 4 to 5 hours or until the pork is very tender. Remove from the oven and allow to cool until the meat can be handled.

Remove the meat from the pot and set the pot aside. Place the pork on a large cutting board and, using two forks, shred into pieces. Discard the bones and any fat. Place the shredded meat on a large baking sheet.

Preheat oven to 425 degrees F.

Skim the fat from the cooking liquid, then boil over high heat until reduced by half. Pour enough of the reduced liquid over the meat to moisten it well without making it soupy.

Place the baking sheet in the oven and roast for about 20 minutes or until the top is beginning to dry and brown. Stir and return to the oven for another 20 minutes.

Serve with warm tortillas, pico de gallo, guacamole, and *refritos*.

SERVES 6   *Simple Braised Beef*

¼ cup butter

3 tablespoons extra-
virgin olive oil

1 onion, finely chopped

2 carrots, finely chopped

1 celery rib, finely chopped

1 eye of round roast,
2 ½–3 pounds

1 teaspoon salt

½ teaspoon pepper

1 cup dry red wine

1 ripe tomato, peeled
and chopped

1 can (14 ½ ounces)
diced tomatoes

1 tablespoon tomato paste

¼ cup warm water

4 cups beef stock

You can create this in the slow cooker, but it's much richer and more flavorful braised in the oven.

Preheat oven to 300 degrees F.

In a Dutch oven or braising pan, heat the butter and oil over medium-high heat. Add the onion, carrots, and celery. Reduce heat and cook for about 10 minutes, stirring occasionally.

Add the roast and brown on all sides. Sprinkle with salt and pepper, then add the wine and cook until it evaporates. Add the tomatoes. Mix the tomato paste and warm water in a small bowl, then add to the pot. Stir in enough beef stock to cover at least half the roast. Cover and place the pan in the lower third of the oven. After about 30 minutes, check to see that the liquid is barely simmering. If it's boiling, reduce oven temperature by 10 degrees.

Allow to cook for about 1 ½ hours. Remove pan from the oven and remove the roast to a warmed serving platter. Tent with foil to keep warm. Strain the braising liquid and return to the pan. On the stove top, bring to a simmer and cook until sauce is slightly thickened and reduced.

Slice the roast across the grain and pour the sauce over to serve.

Slow Cooker Variation: Brown the vegetables and beef as directed. Place in the slow cooker. Deglaze the pan with the wine, scraping up the browned bits. Add the liquid to the cooker along with the salt and pepper, tomatoes, tomato paste, and beef stock. Cook on low for 6 hours.

Remove the roast from the cooker to a warm serving platter, then tent to keep warm. Strain the liquid from the cooker into a small skillet and simmer until slightly thickened and reduced.

Slice the roast across the grain and pour the sauce over to serve.

SERVES 4 | *Ale-Braised Short Ribs with Jalapeño Molasses Glaze*

Bone-in short ribs,
3 ½–4 pounds

Salt

Black pepper

2 tablespoons extra-virgin
olive oil

2 large yellow onions, quartered

2 large carrots, cut into
1-inch chunks

1 bottle (12 ounces) amber ale

1 cup beef stock

2 fresh rosemary sprigs

2 bay leaves

¼ cup molasses

1 jalapeño, finely chopped

Braising is a good technique for short ribs because they become so tender they fall from the bone. Use beef or bison, whichever you prefer; just make sure they're bone-in.

Preheat oven to 300 degrees F.

Pat the ribs dry and sprinkle with salt and pepper. Heat the oil in a large Dutch oven over medium-high heat. Brown the ribs on all sides in batches so that they don't crowd each other in the pot. Place in a single layer on a platter.

When all of the ribs have been browned, discard all but one tablespoon of fat from the pot and return to heat. Add the onions and carrots and sauté until the onions become translucent, about 5 minutes. Pour in the ale and bring to a boil, scraping the bottom of the pot to loosen the browned bits. Add the stock and return to a boil for 2 more minutes. Reduce the heat to low and return the ribs to the pot. Pour in any collected juices from the platter. The ribs should be mostly submerged in the liquid. Add more ale or water if necessary. Add the rosemary and bay leaves.

If there's too much headspace in the pot, cover it with parchment so that the paper is almost touching the meat. Leave about an inch of overhang outside of the pot. Cover tightly with the lid and place in the oven. After 15 minutes, check to see that the liquid is at a low simmer. If it's boiling, reduce the oven temperature by about 10 degrees F. Braise for 2 ½ hours or until the meat falls from the bone, turning the ribs every 45 minutes.

Meanwhile, make the glaze. Bring the molasses to a gentle boil. Add the jalapeño and cook for about 2 minutes. Remove from heat, cover, and allow to stand until the ribs are ready, at least 1 hour.

When the ribs are done, remove the pot from the oven. Lift the ribs from the pot and place them on a baking sheet in a single layer. Tent with foil to keep warm.

Using a slotted spoon, remove the vegetables from the pot and discard. Place the pot on the burner and skim off most of the fat. Turn heat to medium-high and boil for about 15 minutes or until liquid is reduced to about ½ cup. Add salt and pepper to taste. Keep warm.

Heat the broiler to high. Brush the ribs with the glaze. Place under the broiler until they begin to sizzle. Remove and transfer to serving plates. Pour a little of the reduced liquid around them.

| *Chipotle Beef Burritos*

1 boneless chuck roast, 4 pounds

1 teaspoon salt

1 teaspoon ground black pepper

2 tablespoons vegetable oil

1 large onion, chopped

5 cloves garlic, minced

1 ½ cups roasted, peeled, and chopped green chiles

1 small can chipotles in *adobo* sauce, finely chopped

8 fresh Roma tomatoes, seeded and chopped

2 cups beef broth

12 large flour tortillas

Sour cream, for garnish (optional)

Chopped lettuce, for garnish (optional)

Red chile sauce, for garnish (page 75, optional)

A variation on carne seca *(dried beef), you can turn these into chimichangas by frying the burritos in oil until golden brown. Smother with chile verde instead of enchilada sauce, if you desire.*

Preheat oven to 300 degrees F.

Trim the roast of any excess fat, dry with a paper towel, and sprinkle all over with salt and pepper. Heat the oil in a braising pan over medium-high heat. Brown the roast on all sides.

Add the onion, garlic, green chiles, chipotles with *adobo* sauce, tomatoes, and beef broth to the pan. Cover the pan with parchment almost touching the meat and extending beyond the rim of the pan. Place the lid on the pan and set in the lower one-third of the oven. After 15 minutes, check to be sure the liquid is gently simmering. If it's boiling too quickly, lower the oven temperature 10 degrees. Braise 2 ½–3 hours, or until the meat is tender, turning once after the first hour. Remove from the oven and allow to cool. This step can be done in advance. Refrigerate for up to two days.

Using two forks, shred the beef. If too much liquid remains, place the pan over medium-high heat and cook until dry, stirring to keep from sticking or burning.

Wrap the tortillas in foil and warm in the oven. Place a heaping amount of meat on the edge of each tortilla, fold in the edges, and roll. Place seam-side-down on a plate and garnish with lettuce, sour cream, or slightly warmed red chile sauce, if desired.

Slow Cooker Variation: Brown the roast as directed and place in the slow cooker. Add the onion, garlic, green chiles, chipotles with *adobo* sauce, tomatoes, and beef broth. Cover and cook on high for 6 hours checking to make sure there is always at least a small amount of liquid in the bottom. Reduce heat to low and continue cooking for 2 to 4 hours or until the meat is tender. Shred and turn into burritos as directed.

SERVES 4 | *Buffalo Osso Bucco*

4 buffalo shanks

Salt and pepper

¼ cup flour

4 tablespoons vegetable oil

1 cup chopped onion

3 ribs celery, chopped

3 carrots, chopped

1 ½ cups chopped tomatoes

Pinch of salt

1 cup dry white wine

2 cups veal or beef stock
(pages 11, 12)

1 bay leaf

2 teaspoons chopped
fresh rosemary

1 tablespoon chopped fresh
thyme

2 tablespoons grated lemon zest

2 tablespoons finely
minced parsley

2 cloves garlic, finely minced

Osso Bucco is an Italian specialty usually prepared with veal, but in the West, buffalo is a healthy alternative. Serve it with a risotto or the polenta recipe that follows. Finish it off with a sprinkle of gremolata, *a blend of lemon zest, parsley, and garlic.*

Preheat oven to 300 degrees F.

Salt and pepper the shanks on all sides and then dredge in flour. Use a piece of kitchen twine to tie the meat to the bone of each shank. Heat the oil over high heat in a Dutch oven. Add the shanks and brown well on all sides. Remove to a plate.

Add the onion, celery, and carrots to the Dutch oven and sauté until tender, stirring frequently. Add the tomatoes and a pinch of salt and cook for another 2 minutes. Add the wine and deglaze the pan, scraping the browned bits from the bottom. Return the shanks to the pot and stir in the stock, bay leaf, rosemary, and thyme.

Cover with a heavy lid and place in the oven. Check after about 15 minutes. If the liquid is boiling, reduce the oven temperature by 10 degrees. Braise for 2 ½–3 hours until the meat is tender.

Just before the meat is finished, make the *gremolata*: mix together the lemon zest, parsley, and garlic in a small bowl. Set aside. (Continued on page 122).

Remove the pan from the oven and place the meat on a warm platter. Tent with foil to keep warm. Heat the braising liquid over high heat on the stove top until slightly reduced.

To serve, remove the string from each shank and place each on a bed of creamy Cheesy Polenta (recipe follows), pour over some sauce, and sprinkle with the *gremolata*.

SERVES 8 | ## Cheesy Polenta

---

2 cups water

1 cup polenta or finely ground cornmeal

½ teaspoon salt

¼ teaspoon pepper

¼ cup butter

½ cup grated Parmesan cheese

Marinara sauce

Polenta is a staple in Italian cooking. It can be served creamy or baked. It's also good the next day fried in a small bit of butter.

Bring the water to a boil in a large saucepan. Pour in the polenta in a steady stream, stirring constantly. Bring to a boil again and then immediately reduce heat and continue to stir until the polenta is thickened and begins to pull away from the sides of the pan, about 20 minutes. Add the salt and pepper, then stir in the butter and cheese. Continue to stir until the butter and cheese are melted, adding a little water if the polenta is too thick. For a creamy polenta, scoop onto plates immediately and serve. For a firmer polenta, pour into a buttered baking dish and bake at 300 degrees F for 15 minutes or until lightly browned. Cut into squares and serve with marinara sauce.

Braised Venison

SERVES 6

1 ½ cups dry red wine

6 cloves garlic, pressed

1 tablespoon dry mustard

1 tablespoon dried rosemary

1 tablespoon dried thyme

1 venison roast, 3 pounds

10 jalapeño-stuffed green olives

10 cloves garlic

¼ pound salt pork, cut into small strips

¼ cup extra-virgin olive oil

1 large onion, sliced

1 ½ cups dry red wine

1 can (28 ounces) Italian tomatoes

1 bay leaf

2 sprigs fresh thyme

2 sprigs fresh rosemary

1 teaspoon salt

½ teaspoon pepper

Venison can sometimes be tough, dry, and strongly flavored, but a long marinade followed by a slow braise with aromatic vegetables makes it moist and tender.

In a small bowl, whisk together the red wine, garlic, mustard, rosemary, and thyme. Place the roast in a large plastic zipper bag and pour the marinade over. Refrigerate for 24–48 hours, turning frequently.

Remove the roast from the marinade and pat dry. Make small slits in the sides of the roast and tuck the stuffed olives, garlic cloves, and strips of salt pork into the slits. Allow to sit at room temperature for 30 minutes.

Preheat oven to 300 degrees F. In a large Dutch oven or braising pan, heat the olive oil over medium-high heat. Add the onion and cook until soft and fragrant, about 8 minutes. Remove from the pan and add the roast. Brown on all sides and then remove. Add the red wine to the pan and deglaze, scraping up the browned bits. Return the onions and the roast to the pan. Add the tomatoes, bay leaf, thyme, rosemary, salt, and pepper. Bring to a boil and then cover with a heavy lid.

Place the pan in the oven and braise for 3–4 hours until the meat is tender. Check after 15 minutes to make sure that the liquid is at a gentle simmer. Reduce heat by 10 degrees F if necessary.

Remove from the oven and place the roast on a warm serving platter. Tent with foil to keep warm. Strain the braising liquid and return to the pan. Bring to a boil over high heat until reduced. Pour over the roast to serve.

SERVES 2–4 | *Pheasant in White Wine Sauce*

I pheasant, 3–5 pounds,
cleaned and cut into pieces

2 cups dry white wine

2 bay leaves

I clove garlic, pressed

I small onion, minced

2 cups chicken stock

3–5 tablespoons vegetable oil

I medium-size sweet
onion, sliced

I teaspoon salt

½ teaspoon pepper

4 sprigs fresh thyme

I bay leaf

Young, farm-raised birds are available in high-end meat markets. Smaller birds are usually more tender and moist.

Place the pheasant pieces in a large zippered plastic storage bag. Combine I cup of the white wine, bay leaves, garlic, onion, and I cup of the chicken stock. Pour over the pheasant, seal the bag and refrigerate for 24 hours, turning the bag often.

Heat 3 tablespoons of oil over medium-high heat in a Dutch oven. Add the pheasant pieces, taking care not to crowd the pan. Brown on all sides until golden. Remove from the pan and add more oil if needed. When the pheasant pieces are browned, add the sweet onion to the pan and sauté until soft, about 5 minutes. Add the remaining cup of wine to the pan and deglaze, stirring and scraping the browned bits from the bottom. Add the pheasant pieces, pour over the remaining cup of chicken stock, season with salt and pepper, and add the thyme and bay leaf.

Reduce heat until the liquid barely simmers, cover the pan, and cook for about I hour or until the pheasant is tender. Remove the pheasant pieces from the pan and tent to keep warm. Bring the liquid in the pot to a boil and cook until reduced by half. Remove the thyme and bay leaf and pour the sauce over the pheasant.

Serve with wild rice.

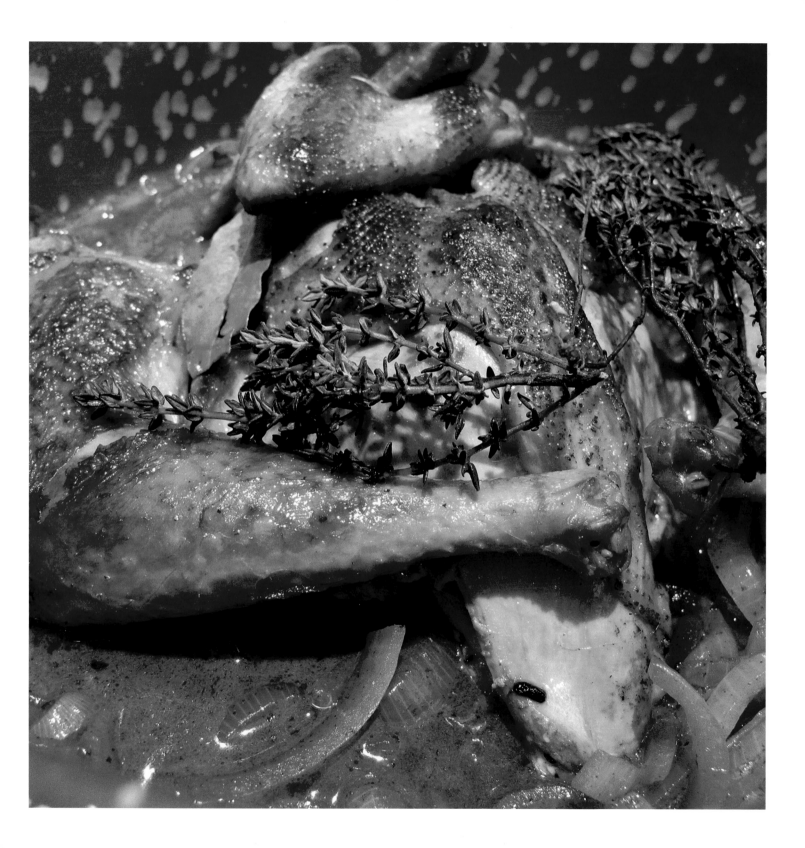

| SERVES 4 | *Braised Rabbit with Brandied Prunes* |

1 fresh rabbit, about
3 pounds, cut up

2 cups red wine

¼ cup chopped fresh parsley

2 tablespoons chopped
fresh rosemary

2 tablespoons chopped
fresh thyme

1 clove garlic, minced

12 pitted prunes

½ cup brandy

½ cup boiling water

2 slices thick-cut
bacon, chopped

4 carrots, cut into 1-inch pieces

3 ribs celery, chopped

1 large onion, minced

1 cup sliced fresh mushrooms

1 teaspoon salt

1 teaspoon black pepper

1 cup red wine

Farm-raised rabbit is generally preferable to wild rabbit because the meat is more tender and mildly flavored. You can find rabbit at gourmet grocery stores or through online sources (see Sources, page 142).

Place the rabbit pieces in a large zippered bag. Combine 1 cup red wine, parsley, rosemary, thyme, and garlic in a small bowl. Pour over the rabbit in the bag. Seal and marinate 4 hours.

Preheat the oven to 300 degrees F. Remove the rabbit from the marinade, reserving the liquid.

Place the prunes in a heat-proof bowl and pour the brandy and boiling water over them. Set aside.

In a Dutch oven or braising pan, cook the bacon until crisp and then remove. Add the rabbit pieces and brown on all sides. Remove. Pour any remaining bacon grease from the pan. Add the marinating liquid to the pan and stir to deglaze, scraping up any browned bits on the bottom. Remove from heat. Return the bacon and the rabbit to the pan. Add the carrots, celery, onions, and mushrooms. Sprinkle with salt and pepper and pour the remaining red wine over all. Cover the pan with parchment almost touching the meat and overlapping the edges of the pan. Place the lid on the pan and set in the lower one-third of the oven. After 15 minutes, check to see that liquid is lightly simmering. If it's boiling hard, reduce heat 10 degrees.

Braise for 1 ½ hours. Drain the reserved prunes and add to the pan. Cover and continue to braise another 30 minutes. Remove from oven.

Place the rabbit, prunes, and vegetables on a warmed serving platter and tent with foil to keep warm. Over medium heat, reduce the braising liquid by half. Pour over the platter before serving.

SERVES 6–8 | *Javelina Stew*

I javelina shoulder,
about 3 pounds

I can (28 ounces) vegetable
juice, such as V-8

6 cloves garlic, minced

I onion, minced

3 teaspoons salt

2 teaspoons black pepper

2 tablespoons vegetable oil

I large yellow onion,
thinly sliced

6 cloves garlic, coarsely chopped

2 large green bell peppers,
seeded and sliced

I large red bell pepper,
seeded and sliced

3 jalapeños, seeded
and chopped

2 cups beer

I teaspoon dried oregano

3 tablespoons chile powder

I teaspoon cayenne pepper

I tablespoon cumin seeds

I can (28 ounces) stewed
tomatoes, drained

I tablespoon flour
(for slow cooker variation)

The javelina, or collared peccary, is a common game animal in Arizona, New Mexico, and Texas. They resemble small pigs, although they belong to a different genus, and move in herds. The trick to cooking javelina is to make sure the hunter who supplies it knows how to deal with the skin and the musk gland. There's nothing worse than cooking poorly prepared javelina, which has an overpowering pungent odor and taste. Good javelina, however, is a popular dish throughout the Southwest, especially in rural areas where hunting is a popular sport.

Place the javelina shoulder in a large zippered plastic bag or in a large glass dish. Combine the vegetable juice, garlic, onion, I teaspoon salt, and I teaspoon pepper and pour over the meat. Allow to marinate in the refrigerator for 24–48 hours, turning occasionally.

Place the cumin in a small skillet over high heat. Shake until the cumin is lightly toasted and fragrant. Remove from the skillet and set aside.

Preheat oven to 300 degrees F. In a heavy braising pot over medium-high heat, sauté the onion, garlic, green and red bell peppers, and jalapeños in the oil until the vegetables are soft and fragrant.

Drain the marinade from the meat and discard. Place the meat in the braising pot with the vegetables. Pour the beer over all. Add the oregano, chile powder, cayenne pepper, cumin seeds, and stewed tomatoes, along with 2 teaspoons salt and I teaspoon pepper, and stir. Tightly cover the pot and place in the oven. Braise for 3–4 hours until the meat is tender and falls from the bone. Remove from the oven.

Remove the meat and vegetables from the pot. Shred the meat and discard the bone. Tent with foil to keep warm. Place the pot over medium-high heat and boil until the sauce is reduced by half. Return the meat and vegetables and stir well until heated through.

Slow Cooker Variation: Marinate the meat as directed. Sauté the vegetables and add to the slow cooker with the drained meat. Pour in the beer and add the oregano, chile powder, cayenne pepper, cumin seeds, stewed tomatoes, salt and pepper. Stir to mix. Cover and cook on low for 6–8 hours. Remove the meat and shred. Remove about one cup of the juice from the slow cooker and whisk in a tablespoon of flour. Pour back into the cooker and stir to thicken. Return the meat to the cooker, cover, and cook on high for another 30 minutes.

Serve in bowls with warm flour tortillas.

Desserts

SERVES 12–15 | *Orange Flan*

1 ½ cups sugar

8 eggs

2 cans (14 ounces each) sweetened condensed milk (not evaporated)

1 ¼ cups whole milk

1 teaspoon vanilla

1 teaspoon orange extract

¼ teaspoon salt

2 tablespoons Grand Marnier or other orange liqueur

2 cans mandarin oranges, drained, for garnish

Raspberries, for garnish

A great party dessert, especially after a spicy meal.

Preheat the oven to 325 degrees F.

Pour the sugar into a heavy, medium-sized skillet. Place the skillet over medium heat until the sugar begins to melt. Reduce the heat to low and, without stirring, allow the sugar to melt and turn golden brown. Working quickly, pour the resulting caramel over the bottom of a 3-quart glass baking dish, tilting to spread up the sides.

In a large bowl, whisk the eggs until blended and then whisk in the sweetened condensed milk, whole milk, vanilla, orange extract, salt, and liqueur. Blend until smooth. Strain the mixture into the prepared baking dish. Cover the dish with foil. Place a large roasting pan of warm water on the oven's middle rack. Set the baking dish into the roasting pan. The water must reach half the depth of the baking dish.

Bake for 1 ½ hours until the center feels just firm when pressed. Remove from the water bath and allow to cool. Refrigerate until serving.

To serve, run a knife around the edges of the baking dish. Place a large serving platter over the dish and turn both upside down. Gently shake the dish to release the flan. Use the drained mandarin slices to create flowers on the top of the flan, using the raspberries for the centers.

| ## Chocolate Cherry Bread Pudding

6 cups cubed (1-inch) challah or brioche, dried overnight

8 ounces premium dark chocolate, cut into small chunks

1 cup dried cherries

2 cups half-and-half

6 eggs

¼ cup sugar

1 teaspoon vanilla extract

1 teaspoon cinnamon

Whipped cream, for garnish

Even in the middle of summer when it feels too hot to turn on the oven, you can serve an elegant dessert by using your slow cooker.

Spray the inside of a slow cooker with nonstick cooking spray. Place half of the bread cubes in the bottom. Sprinkle with half of the chocolate and cherries. Cover with the remaining bread cubes, then top with the remaining chocolate and cherries.

In a medium bowl, whisk together the half-and-half, eggs, sugar, vanilla, and cinnamon until well blended. Pour evenly over the bread mixture in the cooker. Cover with plastic wrap and set a heavy plate on top to make sure the bread stays submerged for about 30 minutes.

Remove the weight and plastic wrap. Cover and cook on high for about 1 ½ hours or until set. Let stand for about 5 to 10 minutes before serving. Serve garnished with whipped cream.

SERVES 8

Blueberry Peach Cobbler

10 cups peeled and sliced fresh peaches

1 pint fresh blueberries

½ cup sugar, depending on sweetness of peaches

1 teaspoon vanilla

2 tablespoons lemon juice

3 tablespoons flour

½ teaspoon powdered ginger

1 tablespoon butter

1 cup plus 1 tablespoon flour

1 cup sugar

1 teaspoon baking powder

¼ teaspoon salt

1 egg

1 cup evaporated milk

½ cup melted butter, slightly cooled

Vanilla ice cream, for garnish

Around my house, it's not summer until we enjoy this delicious cobbler made with fresh Colorado peaches from the farmers market.

Preheat oven to 425 degrees F. Spray a 3-quart baking dish with cooking spray.

In a large bowl, gently combine peaches, blueberries, sugar, vanilla, lemon juice, flour, and ginger. Pour into the prepared dish and dot with 1 tablespoon of butter. Bake uncovered until hot and bubbly, about 45 minutes.

Just before the fruit is finished, make the topping. Combine the flour, sugar, baking powder, and salt in a large bowl. In a separate bowl, beat together the egg, milk, and butter. Add the liquids to the flour mixture and stir until combined, taking care not to overmix.

Remove the fruit from the oven and reduce temperature to 375 degrees F. Pour the topping over the fruit and place back in the oven. Bake for another 45 minutes or until topping is slightly puffed and golden brown.

Serve warm with a scoop of premium vanilla ice cream.

| ## *Brandied Pecan Pie*

½ cup pecan pieces

1 ¼ cups all-purpose flour

2 tablespoons sugar

½ cup butter, chilled and cut into chunks

2 tablespoons ice water

1 teaspoon brandy

3 large eggs

1 cup sugar

¾ cup light corn syrup

2 tablespoons butter, melted

2 teaspoons vanilla extract

¼ cup brandy

¼ teaspoon salt

2 cups pecan halves

Whipped cream or vanilla ice cream, for garnish

Every fall, my Uncle Walt and Aunt Shirley would harvest pecans from their southern Arizona trees, lovingly shell the nuts by hand, and give them to us for Christmas. If you can find fresh pecans, use them. The flavor is so much more pronounced than in the bagged version you find in the grocery store.

Make the crust: Pulse pecan pieces in a food processor until finely chopped. Add flour and sugar to processor and pulse to combine. Add butter and pulse until crumbly. With the processor running, pour in the water and brandy. Process just until dough begins to form a ball.

Remove from the processor and shape the dough into a smooth ball. Cover in plastic wrap and chill for 30 minutes.

On a flour-covered board or a pastry mat, roll the dough into a circle big enough to fit into a 9-inch pie plate at ¼-inch thickness. Line a pie plate with the dough, trim the edges and crimp. Refrigerate for 30 minutes.

Preheat the oven to 350 degrees F. Bake for 55 minutes or until set.

Make the filling: Stir together the eggs, sugar, corn syrup, butter, vanilla, brandy, and salt until well blended. Reserve ½ cup of the pecans and stir the rest into the egg mixture. Pour the filling into the prepared piecrust. Arrange the remaining pecan halves in an attractive pattern on top of the pie.

Serve warm or cold with a dollop of whipped cream or a scoop of vanilla ice cream.

| *Chocolate Chile Fondue*

24 ounces premium dark chocolate, chopped

1 cup heavy cream

1 tablespoon red chile powder

Chunks of assorted fruits such as bananas, apples, pineapple, and berries for dipping

Cubes of pound cake and marshmallows, for dipping

Shortbread cookies, for dipping

A fun dinner party dessert that allows your guests to be creative. The chile adds just a little heat to the sweetness of the chocolate. Be sure to use quality chocolate.

Place the chocolate and cream in a slow cooker and cook on low for 30 minutes or until chocolate is melted. Stir well and add chile powder. Cook another 30 minutes.

To serve, place the slow cooker in the middle of the serving table. Surround with plates of fruit, cake, marshmallows, and cookies along with wooden skewers. Guests can spear and dip their favorites.

Baked Apples with Honey Yogurt Sauce

SERVES 4

4 large red apples, Gala, Fuji, or Braeburn

I slice lemon

2 tablespoons butter, melted and slightly cooled

¼ cup brown sugar, firmly packed

½ cup almonds, toasted and chopped

¼ cup golden raisins

I teaspoon cinnamon

I teaspoon vanilla

½ cup plain yogurt

I tablespoon honey

I teaspoon vanilla extract

A satisfying end to a fall dinner. Put the apples in the oven just before you serve the main course and they'll be ready to serve at dessert time.

Preheat oven to 375 degrees F. Spray a 9 x 9 x 2-inch baking pan with cooking spray.

Core the apples and peel about I inch around the tops. Rub the slice of lemon around the tops. Place the whole, cored apples in the baking pan.

In a small bowl, mix the butter, brown sugar, almonds, raisins, cinnamon, and vanilla. Stuff each of the apples with ¼ of the nut mixture.

Place in the oven and bake until the apples are tender, about 45 minutes.

While the apples are baking, in a small bowl mix the yogurt, honey, and vanilla. Chill until serving time.

Remove the apples from the oven and allow to cool for about 10 minutes. Place one apple on each of four serving plates and top with a generous portion of the yogurt sauce. Serve immediately.

Chocolate Pear Cake

4 ripe pears, peeled, cored, and cut into 1-inch cubes

2 tablespoons butter

¼ cup brown sugar, firmly packed

1 teaspoon ground cinnamon

Additional butter for greasing pan

¾ cup all-purpose flour

½ cup finely ground toasted almonds

¼ cup cocoa powder

½ teaspoon baking powder

½ teaspoon baking soda

4 tablespoons butter, softened

¾ cup sugar

1 teaspoon vanilla extract

2 eggs

⅓ cup milk

4 ounces premium bittersweet chocolate, finely chopped

½ cup heavy cream

¼ cup light corn syrup

2 tablespoons pear liqueur, such as Poire William

This is one of my favorite chocolate cake recipes. It's rich and elegant, yet simple to make.

Sauté the pears, butter, brown sugar, and ½ teaspoon cinnamon over medium heat until the pears are coated and tender, about 4 minutes. Set aside.

Preheat oven to 350 degrees F. Butter a 9-inch round baking pan, line the bottom with parchment, and then butter the parchment.

Sift together the flour, almonds, cocoa powder, baking powder, baking soda, and the remaining ½ teaspoon of cinnamon. In a separate bowl, cream the softened 4 tablespoons of butter. Add the sugar and beat until fluffy. Add the vanilla and eggs, beating well. Gradually add the flour mixture, stirring well after each addition. Fold in the milk and pears. Spread the mixture in the prepared pan and bake until a cake tester comes out clean, approximately 55 minutes.

Make the chocolate sauce: Place the chopped chocolate in a heat-proof bowl. Heat the heavy cream and corn syrup in a saucepan over medium heat until it begins to simmer. Remove from heat and pour half of this mixture over the chocolate. Let it sit for 1 minute, then whisk until the chocolate is melted. Add the remaining cream mixture and stir to blend. (A handheld immersion blender helps to incorporate the melted chocolate into the cream.) Set aside.

Remove the cake from the oven and cool in the pan on a wire rack for 20 minutes. Invert the cake onto serving a plate and remove the parchment. (Continued on next page.)

Allow to cool completely. Just before serving, warm the chocolate sauce and stir in the pear liqueur. Pour over the cake, completely covering the top, and allow the sauce to run down the sides.

SERVES 10

Dulce de Leche Chocolate Trifle

2 quarts whole milk

3 cups sugar

1 vanilla bean

½ teaspoon baking soda

1 ½ cups sugar

1 cup flour

¼ cup cocoa powder

¼ teaspoon salt

12 egg whites at room temperature

1 ½ teaspoons cream of tartar

8 ounces premium bittersweet chocolate, finely chopped

1 cup heavy cream

½ cup light corn syrup

1 quart fresh strawberries

1 pint fresh raspberries

1 pint fresh blackberries

Whipped cream, for garnish

Dulce de leche, a sauce similar to caramel sauce, also makes a popular topping for fruit or ice cream, or add it to hot coffee with a shot of Kahlua.

Make the *dulce de leche*: In a large saucepan, stir together the milk, sugar, and vanilla bean. Bring to a simmer over medium heat, stirring until the sugar is dissolved. Add the baking soda and stir. Reduce heat to low and continue to barely simmer, stirring occasionally, for 1 hour. Remove the vanilla bean and continue to simmer for another hour or so until the liquid is a dark golden brown and thickened and reduced to about 2 cups. Remove from heat and strain. Set aside.

While the *dulce de leche* is cooking, bake the cake. Place oven rack at the lowest position and preheat the oven to 325 degrees F.

Sift together 1 cup of the sugar with the flour, cocoa powder, and salt. In a medium-size bowl, beat the egg whites at medium speed until foamy. Add the cream of tartar and beat at high speed until soft peaks form. Continue beating and gradually add the remaining ½ cup of sugar. Beat until the peaks are firmer, but not stiff. Do not overbeat. Gently fold in the dry ingredients in ¼-cup increments until no streaks remain, taking care not to deflate the

egg whites. Spread into a 10-inch tube pan and bake 50–60 minutes or until the cake is firm and springs back when touched. Remove from the oven, turn upside down, and cool on a rack.

Make the chocolate sauce: Place the chopped chocolate in a heat-proof bowl. Heat the heavy cream and corn syrup in a saucepan over medium heat until it begins to simmer. Remove from heat and pour half of this mixture over the chocolate. Let it sit for 1 minute, then whisk until the chocolate is melted. Add the remaining cream mixture and stir to blend.

To assemble the trifle, wash and dry the fruit and slice the strawberries. Remove the cooled cake from the pan and, using a serrated knife, cut into 1-inch cubes. Place one third of the cake cubes in the bottom of a glass trifle bowl or other clear glass serving bowl. Top with one third of the strawberries, raspberries, and blackberries. Drizzle with warm *dulce de leche* and chocolate sauce. Repeat layers and drizzle the top with remaining sauces.

To serve, spoon into serving bowls and top with a dollop of whipped cream.

MAKES 6 CUPS | *Spiced Applesauce*

12 cups peeled, cored, and
sliced Granny Smith or other
baking apples

½ cup of sugar

1 teaspoon cinnamon

1 teaspoon freshly grated nutmeg

½ teaspoon dried ginger

½ teaspoon allspice

1 cup water

1 tablespoon lemon juice

This makes a chunky applesauce. If you prefer yours without lumps, use a potato masher to smooth them out.

Place the apples in a slow cooker. Combine the sugar, cinnamon, nutmeg, ginger, and allspice. Sprinkle over the apples and toss to coat. Stir in the water and lemon juice. Cover and cook on low for 5–7 hours or on high 2 ½–3 ½ hours. Stir and serve hot or cold.

SERVES 6 | *Arroz con Leche y Chocolate*

2 ½ cups cooked rice

1 ½ cups scalded milk

⅓ cup brown sugar

3 eggs, beaten

6 ounces premium dark
chocolate, melted and
slightly cooled

½ teaspoon salt

2 tablespoons vanilla

1 teaspoon cinnamon

½ teaspoon nutmeg

½ cup raisins

Rice pudding has always been one of my favorite comfort foods, and with chocolate, it's even better.

Coat the slow cooker with nonstick cooking spray. In a large bowl, combine the rice, milk, brown sugar, eggs, chocolate, salt, vanilla, cinnamon, nutmeg, and raisins. Pour into the slow cooker. Cook on high 1 ½–2 hours.

☀ *Sources*

MEATS

Wild Idea Buffalo Company
P.O. Box 1209
Rapid City, South Dakota 57709
(866) 658-6137
www.wildideabuffalo.com
Sustainably raised, native-grassfed
buffalo.

Buffalo Gal
32488 Cody Drive
Houston, Minnesota 55943
(507) 896-2345
www.buffalogal.com
Buffalo and other specialty meat products.

ExoticMeats.com
1003 Northeast Loop 410
San Antonio, Texas 78209
(800) 680-4375
www.exoticmeats.com
The name says it all.

Ranch Foods Direct
2901 North El Paso
Colorado Springs, Colorado 80907
(719) 473-2306
www.ranchfoodsdirect.com
Ranch-raised beef and other meats.

Aravaipa's Painted Cave Cattle Company
P.O. Box 228
Tucson, Arizona 85702

(800) 237-5625
www.tucsonbeef.com
Pasture-raised beef.

BEANS, CORN, CHILES, AND SPICES

Native Seeds/SEARCH
2601 North Campbell
Tucson, Arizona 85719
(866) 622-5561
www.nativeseeds.org
Heirloom varieties of beans, chiles, corn,
spices, and other desert specialties. Also,
heirloom seeds for growing your own.

Rancho Gordo
1924 Yajome Street
Napa, California 94559
(707) 259-1935
www.ranchogordo.com
Heirloom beans, dried corn, dried
chiles and powders, spices, grains.

Santa Fe School of Cooking
116 West San Francisco Street
Santa Fe, New Mexico 87501
(800) 982-4688
www.santafeschoolofcooking.com
Anything you need for Southwest
cooking including chile powders, chiles,
beans, corn, spices, and equipment.

Hatch Chile Express
P.O. Box 350
Hatch, New Mexico 87937

(800) 292-4454
www.hatch-chile.com
From the chile capital of New Mexico,
if not the world, fresh and frozen green
chile, red chile pods, and chile powders.

MEXICAN SPECIALTIES AND INGREDIENTS

MexGrocer.com
4060 Morena Boulevard, Suite C
San Diego, California 92117
(858) 270-0577
www.mexgrocer.com
Mexican spices, foods, kitchen
equipment, and more.

BARBECUE EQUIPMENT AND SUPPLIES

The Barbecue Store
11220 S. Highway 6 #A-4
Sugar Land, Texas 77478
(888) 789-0650
www.barbecue-store.com
Barbecues, thermometers, charcoal,
wood chips, and other equipment
and supplies.

BBQ.com
4117 Rhoda Drive
Baton Rouge, Louisiana 70816
(877) 743-2269
www.bbq.com
Everything you need to barbecue,
smoke, grill, or build an outdoor
kitchen.

Index

About the Author

MARILYN NOBLE, a freelance writer, editor, and personal chef, comes from a long line of great home cooks. Her articles about food, art, travel, and other topics have appeared in print publications around the world and online. She is also the author of *Viva Chocolate!* Marilyn was born and raised in southern Arizona and now makes her home in Colorado where she hikes, gardens, and is a member of the Slow Food Denver leadership group.